Praise for

# ALIGN
# FEEL
# HEAL

"David Starbuck Smith has masterfully blended decades of clinical experience, scientific evidence, and compelling case studies to create a powerful solution to help anyone free themselves from chronic pain. I can personally attest to the fact that he's among the most talented healers I've ever seen."

—Jim Dethmer, bestselling author of *The 15 Commitments of Conscious Leadership*

"David's book is a transformative guide to understanding the profound connection between our emotions, physical health, and posture. It's filled with invaluable insights on how to use the pain in our lives—both emotional and physical—as a compass toward healing and fulfillment. As an orthopedic surgeon with over two decades of experience, I can confidently say this book is essential reading for anyone experiencing musculoskeletal pain. Its wisdom applies not just to those with physical discomfort, but to anyone with chronic health conditions seeking to understand the deep interplay between emotional and physical health. In a world driven by endless distractions and cultural pressures for quick fixes, David's work is a timely and necessary resource for true, lasting wellness."

—Dr. Kian Raiszadeh, MD, QME, IME, Board Certified Orthopedic Surgeon

"As a culture, we've never been more interested in living healthy, active, pain-free lives at any age. But up until now, a key piece of the puzzle has been missing. What we've needed, and what this book provides, is a clear, step-by-step plan to help us live free of pain and limitation, without reliance on drugs and surgery. David Starbuck Smith connects the dots and shows us clearly how we can take control of our physical and emotional selves to live the lives we've imagined."

—Bill Stump, former CEO of Egoscue

"David Starbuck Smith is a profound healer and guide who deeply understands how emotional blockages create pain and disease. In a very clear and practical way, David empowers us to solve long-standing physical issues related to stress in the body."

—Dr. Jennifer Freed, bestselling author of *A Map to Your Soul*

## Praise for
## *Ageless, Painless Tennis*

"David Smith has pulled off a form of magic. In a radical act of alchemy, he has turned simple and effective movements into improved tennis performance. Believe it or not, solving musculoskeletal pain is actually the low bar. Don't be fooled. David is more interested in you playing savage tennis for the rest of your life. This book is a gift that will keep on giving."

—Dr. Kelly Starrett, DPT, coach and *New York Times* bestselling author of *Becoming a Supple Leopard* and *Ready to Run: Unlocking Your Potential to Run Naturally*

"David has masterfully captured cutting-edge principles to achieve physical and mental wellness that will keep you pain-free and active for a lifetime."

—Jeff Greenwald, MFT, author of *The Best Tennis of Your Life* and two-time world champion

"A must-read for weekend warriors and advanced athletes alike looking to heal nagging injuries and prevent future ones!"

—Brad Gilbert, former world #4, coach, ESPN tennis analyst, and author of *Winning Ugly*

*Align, Feel, Heal:*
*An Integrated Solution to Eliminating Chronic Pain at Its Roots*
by David Starbuck Smith

© Copyright 2025 David Starbuck Smith

979-8-88824-711-2

All rights reserved. No part of this publication may be reproduced, stored in a retrieval system, or transmitted in any form or by any means—electronic, mechanical, photocopy, recording, or any other—except for brief quotations in printed reviews, without the prior written permission of the author.

Published by

3705 Shore Drive
Virginia Beach, VA 23455
800-435-4811
www.koehlerbooks.com

# ALIGN
# FEEL
# HEAL

An Integrated Solution to
Eliminating Chronic Pain
at Its Roots

## DAVID STARBUCK SMITH

VIRGINIA BEACH
CAPE CHARLES

# Before Your Journey Begins

At times, this book will ask you to grab a shovel and dig deep. Digging up a buried past and making it present isn't always comfortable or easy. Yet, with every layer of dirt you remove, you bring yourself closer to freedom.

If you hit a few rocks along the way, keep digging if you're able. If you run into a rock that's too difficult to budge and requires an extra set of hands, then always ask for help.

Often, emotional pain and trauma aren't mere specks of dirt that can be easily brushed off your shoulder. Sometimes, they can make you feel like you're the one who's buried. If that's the case, I suggest contacting your most trusted emotional health counselor or professional who can help you navigate your way back to the surface so that you may breathe freely once again.

Similarly, if you're suffering from a physical pain or ailment and need to contact a health practitioner before, during, or after you launch into the pages and exercises inside, please do. Although this book might be considered "self-help," sometimes, helping yourself requires asking for the help you need rather than trying to do it all on your own.

Remember that all healing comes from within, no matter the modality, medication, procedure, book, or professional you enlist on your healing journey. I hope this book ignites that healing light and then continues to fuel the fire inside so that you may realize your very best health in body, mind, and life.

# Introduction

THERE'S A SAYING that goes: "You have a million dreams when you're healthy, but when you're in pain, you only have one." I'm sure the 1.5 billion people in the world who suffer from chronic pain every year would agree. I can also relate both personally and professionally. Over the last several decades, I've worked with thousands of people with just about every painful muscle, nerve, and joint condition that exists. I've worked with two-year-old kids, ninety-five-year-old great-grandmothers, athletes of every level in just about every sport, and people just like you and me. Pain has a way of separating people from themselves, their loved ones, and their lives, which is something I know all too well.

After transitioning from college tennis to professional tennis in my early twenties, I found myself crippled with debilitating back spasms that would drop me to the ground, intolerable sciatic nerve referral, and a relentless ache in my lower back when standing. I craved relief, but I would have settled for some answers to two questions in particular:

1. What was causing the pain?
2. Why wasn't I healing?

Unfortunately, nobody seemed to know the answers to either question, including the doctors, leaving me feeling irreparably broken and confused. Thirty years later, I now understand why the doctors and trainers didn't have answers for me. They confused the "what" (the symptom) with the "why" (the cause). It's understandable. We all accumulate a lifetime of injuries, colds, and fleeting illnesses; it's part of being human. Ninety-nine percent of the time, we get over them, and doctors never have to question why they happened. Our inner healing superpower takes over and saves the day. Then there are the few aches that stick around like annoying houseguests who long overstay their welcome, like the one in my back. That's when the why begins to matter.

The how is easy. You bent over to pick up a suitcase when your back went out; you let yourself become too worn down and caught the flu; you reached into the backseat of your car when you strained your shoulder; you slept wrong and woke up with a kink in your neck. The explanations for how we got sick or injured are endless and usually effortless.

The why can be much more elusive.

Nobody ever told me why I strained both hips, why I had bone spurs in my ankles, or why I pulled my hamstring during a standard move on the tennis court. I didn't ask either, because it all healed. But when my back didn't respond to stretching my hamstrings and strengthening my core (more on this later) or any of the other traditional treatments for low-back pain, I eventually realized the "experts" didn't know why my lower back hurt.

Of course, plenty of diagnoses were thrown my way: Facet syndrome, disc herniation, arthritis, etc., but they don't explain the why either; they only put a name to the condition without explaining how it got there.

At that point, in my early twenties and facing the prospect of living my life hampered by pain, I decided I wouldn't stop until I found some answers. So, I dove into anatomy, physiology, and biomechanics at UC Berkeley, thinking medical school was my next step and best option. Then, I realized all the doctors I had been to for my pain, although well-meaning, were all trained the same way and, therefore, thought the same way. I needed out-of-the-box thinking, so I found some of the best nontraditional mentors in musculoskeletal pain and joint mechanics on the planet and eventually solved my back pain.

How did I solve my pain? I'll tell you exactly how in the upcoming chapters, but the short answer is that I discovered my why. I'll also help you discover yours so that you may put some of your questions and your pain to rest.

My quest for answers set me on a journey that continues to this day, and for well over twenty years as a postural and exercise therapist, I've been treating people with chronic muscle and joint pain of all kinds so that maybe they, too, can live their lives free of pain and physical limitation.

Since my early twenties, I've also immersed myself in metaphysics, psychology, Zen, meditation, psychological and emotional counseling, quantum physics, and anything and everything related to personal growth. First, I wanted to become more mentally tough on the tennis court, and then I wanted to learn how to free my mind and body to live a happier, healthier life. Now, I help people with their bodies and their lives, and unsurprisingly, the two are intricately intertwined.

For example, I learned my back pain wasn't solely a result of a muscle imbalance in my hips and spine but also a manifestation of suppressed emotional pain I hadn't released. Specifically, I discovered I was carrying a heavy burden in the form of fear. Fear I would fail, fear I would succeed, and underneath all that, fear I would disappoint my family.

Once I formed a connection between my backache and my emotional baggage, I came to wonder just how related other people's emotional passengers were to their physical pain.

After all, the excellent doctors and others in the Western medical model don't typically tell you your neck pain can be related to feeling responsible for everyone else's happiness or that your back pain can reflect a deep fear that you're a disappointment to your parents. They tell you to rest, stretch, try physical therapy, medicate yourself, or, if it comes to it, undergo surgery.

That got me thinking about my clients. With dozens of people seeking help in my clinic every day, I began wondering if they, too, were carrying pockets of emotional energy that were being expressed as physical pain.

As I looked deeper into their lives for a connection, I realized that while I could almost always pinpoint a postural and mechanical imbalance contributing to their symptoms, there was almost always unresolved emotional stress underneath that needed to be acknowledged and released.

This discovery explained why many of my clients had recurring pain and why the pain would show up during stressful times in their lives. It became clear that if an emotional stressor was ignored or remained unhealed, it could continue to act like an on-an-off switch for the pain while sabotaging other parts of their lives in the process, like their relationships, careers, happiness, or overall health.

How does this work? Imagine that you suddenly began to experience nagging pain in your back, recurring colds, or injuries you've never had before. You might blame it on age, but in reality, your symptoms were triggered by powerful feelings of anger, rage, or resentment that were wreaking havoc on your mind and body. Perhaps your life was disrupted by having to care for an aging parent, being under financial strain, or ending a long relationship. I witnessed these exact scenarios many times over the years with many of my clients. They often recovered from their ailment within a few days or weeks, but if they hadn't dealt with the stress in their lives, it wasn't a matter of if, but when they'd be back in my clinic with the same or similar symptoms.

Injuries, autoimmune conditions, various diseases, muscle pain, and joint ailments follow the same playbook. Your physical body is inextricably linked to your emotional state. You may not have equated your last flu, strep throat, back spasm, or Achilles tendon tear to a concurrent stressful event in your life or with painful memories that recently resurfaced, but I hope by the end of this book, you'll at the very least consider the correlation.

So, what's the solution? To end the onslaught of physical

symptoms, you need to rid yourself of the taxing emotional stowaways secretly sabotaging your physical and mental health. You'll also need to balance your muscles, bones, and joints with a few essential techniques and exercises.

There is one catch. Although physical pain and illness are often related to or rooted in past or present emotional pain, we've learned our whole lives to avoid feeling painful emotions at all costs. We often bury them so that we don't have to feel them at all.

So, your task is to bravely expose these buried pockets of destructive emotional energy that are relentlessly gnawing at your body and your life.

You'll do this via targeted stretching and strengthening exercises, meditations, breathing techniques, and thought-provoking journal questions that will help you connect to your body, heart, and soul in a way you may never have before. The reward is that you'll open up the space for your body to tap into its inner wisdom and extraordinary capacity to heal, putting you back in charge of your health and life.

# Part I
*A New Perspective*

## Chapter 1

## BORN TO HEAL

WE ARE BORN to heal. Consider this: We regenerate 330 billion new cells every single day. Our entire bodies—with the exception of brain cells—completely renew over several days, weeks, or months, depending on the type of cell. Our skin cells turn over every month; Our gut microbiome changes every two to four days, and our entire blood supply and the inner lining of our intestines change every two to four weeks. Our bodies are so incredible that we produce four million new red blood cells every single second.

Our capacity to regenerate is why we have healed every injury, illness, ache, pain, cut, and bruise we've ever had until now. In fact, our immune systems are working at this very moment to ward off harmful bacteria, fight infection, and kill cells that could morph into cancer. So, when you add it all up, there is only one obvious conclusion: We are hardwired to heal at every level.

But, if we're magical healers at the core of our being, how does one become trapped in a cycle of chronic pain? That's the billion-dollar question. Is it age, even though plenty of people in their seventies and beyond run marathons, hike, and enjoy their lives unencumbered by pain or a lasting health concern?

Could it be an unfortunate gift passed down by parents, even though epigeneticists are proving our genes are not predestined outcomes but are turned on and off based on our environment?

What about plain, old, bad luck?

We know it doesn't feel like good luck, but let's break it down further: In a general sense, we can say that chronic pain, unlike acute, transitory pain, becomes chronic because something is blocking the body's ability to heal. Simply put, if you're still in pain, it's because the root of the problem hasn't yet been solved, no matter how many medications, surgeries, and health practitioners you've thrown at it. It's like treating a blister on your foot with soothing ointments and Band-Aids without ever freeing your foot from the old, worn-out shoe that's causing it.

It's not your fault. You've followed the standard medical protocol you've been conditioned to follow your whole life. Almost all of us have. Yet, there's something the doctors and pharmaceutical companies don't want you to know: The medical system is neither well-equipped to handle chronic pain nor does it have the solutions you're looking for. How do I know? Because there are still countless millions of people (possibly even you) who have been down that road and are still reeling from the same painful condition they started with years later.

As someone who has been working with chronic pain for over twenty years, I've often wondered how that's possible considering all the modern medical resources at our disposal. To find some answers, I've whittled down the struggle with chronic pain to three essential questions:

1. Why do billions of people in the world continue to suffer from chronic pain each year?
2. Why isn't the traditional model of healthcare helping them solve it?
3. What can one do to find relief?

I'll attempt to answer the first two questions in the upcoming chapters. As for the third, I'll provide a general answer now before we explore several potential avenues of pain relief throughout the book.

I believe the first step to healing is to assume complete and total responsibility for our health, including the pain. What do I mean by that?

As we dive into some neuroscience and the mind-and-body connection, you'll discover that the state of our bodies is much less about our genetics, age, or the activities we do (things out of our control) and much more a reflection of our thoughts, beliefs, habits, and even our emotions—all of which we can assume responsibility for and even consciously change. Therefore, as you read along, I'll ask you to look at yourself in the mirror both literally and figuratively to uncover the physical, mental, and emotional roots of your condition.

In other words, instead of delegating the responsibility of your health to me or another "expert" after all the previous ones have already failed you, I want to make you the expert, thereby placing your health back in your hands where it rightly belongs. Trust me; you want the responsibility of your health in your own hands, because if you leave it up to one person or one system of healthcare, you limit your options and give away your power.

In addition, I firmly believe that pain is there for a reason that serves you. When you discover that reason—the deeper message behind it—you might learn something about yourself that will lead you to better health and greater happiness and fulfillment.

Make no mistake, though, this book isn't magic, and it won't heal you. It's merely a guide. It will be up to you to heal yourself. This is good news because, along the way, you may discover you're not as broken as you thought or have been led to believe. You may even find out where all this pain has really been coming from and that it had nothing to do with age, genetics, or any of the other conventional explanations that are wrong 90 percent of the time.

No matter what, I can guarantee you'll be different than you were before your painful nightmare began. You'll be transformed in a way that only new perspective, awareness, and experience can provide by addressing whatever condition you're dealing with at its roots. By roots, I don't mean your diagnosis, which is simply the term the doctors have used to describe your symptoms (arthritis, chronic fatigue syndrome, degenerative disc disease, etc.). I mean the driving force underneath the symptoms—the real reason for your pain. As you uncover that, you stand to reignite your power to heal. First, though, you need to know what's standing in your way.

## Chapter 2

# A TROUBLING EPIDEMIC

A FORTY-SEVEN-YEAR-OLD MAN named Tim walked into my former clinic in San Francisco some years ago, complaining of persistent radiating pain down the back of his left leg. Tim had been diagnosed with a spinal disc herniation, which occurs when the soft, gooey center of the cushion in between two vertebrae breaks through its outer casing, like jelly leaking from the center of a squashed donut.

In Tim's case, the disc material was pressing against his sciatic nerve, one of two major nerves running from the five lower vertebrae in the spine down the leg. When it's compressed, the symptoms range from numbness and tingling in the feet to a burning sensation along the side or back of the leg. If you've ever experienced sciatic pain, or sciatica, as it's commonly known, then you know how debilitating it can be, and if you haven't, then imagine a constant, painful electrical current running down the back of your thigh.

Over the previous three years, Tim had gone through all the traditional checkpoints, including visits to his general practitioner, followed by an orthopedist, and then a specialized spinal surgeon who ordered the requisite X-rays, an MRI, physical therapy, a cortisone injection, and eventually surgery. Despite his and his healthcare team's best efforts, he still had pain that kept him from exercising, playing with his kids, physical intimacy with his wife, focusing on his work, and enjoying his life. Since the conventional treatments had unsuccessfully run their course and his doctors had run out of answers, they suggested that he would have to learn to "manage" his pain, which is doctor code for: "My tool kit is used up, I'm out of solutions, and you're on your own." Or: "Live with it while staying heavily medicated."

He's not alone. That's how it often goes for nearly one in five of the roughly 1.5 billion people in the world—which includes over 50 million Americans—who experience daily chronic pain. Like Tim, most follow the standard Western medical protocol and shuffle from one doctor or health practitioner to the next, only to run into the same wall and treatment options as the other millions of hopeful souls—medication, physical therapy, and surgeries that may or may not move the needle in their favor. Then, if the typical medical interventions don't succeed, many people become lost and uncertain about where to turn next. If they turn to anything at all. Some are led to believe the pain is imagined or, worse, faked. That's when the seeds of despair begin to sprout.

As one of my clients remarked, "When the doctor told me there was nothing they could do except give me more drugs, I thought, *This can't be my life. I can't possibly live like this.*" Another declared, "I've been everywhere and seen everyone, and nobody seems to be able to help." One woman who had been coping with a frozen shoulder for years said, "I became resigned to the fact that my life would never be the same. I figured I'd just have to live with the limitation." These are common sentiments I've heard almost every day for over twenty years.

I deeply sympathize. The physical hardship is difficult enough as it is, but the mental and emotional toll is often the worst, highlighted by the fact that up to 85 percent of people with chronic pain become depressed at some point. It makes sense, considering that one of the essential components of depression is feeling powerless to change your situation. When we're led to believe there's nothing that can be done by the people we've always trusted to solve our health challenges, it's easy to feel like there's little hope. Yet, depression is only one element in a vicious cascade of physical and emotional turmoil that begins with pain and ends with even more pain.

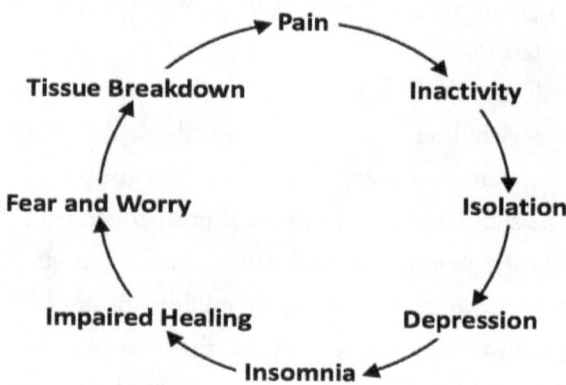

Once the pain has set in, regular activity can become painful or even impossible, leading to a loss of pleasure, endorphins, and enjoyment of life. The inability to do everyday activities and connect to your social circle can be isolating and lonely and often lead to depression. All those things—pain, inactivity, isolation, and depression—individually or combined, can cause insomnia. A lack of sleep impedes the body's ability to regenerate and heal. Fear and worry that the pain won't go away kick off stress hormones that further degrade tissue, which leads to more pain.

Individually, each of these components can lead to an increase in symptoms. Together, they form a debilitating cycle that can spiral out of control.

Unfortunately, that's not all. There are many other unpleasant commonalities almost everyone shares in their struggle:

- Pain emerges in some disabling form and doesn't abate with time, over-the-counter drugs, or intervening therapy.
- It can last for months and even years on end.
- Fear, worry, and anxiety that it won't go away can set in.
- It can be challenging to maintain focus on work.
- Intimate relationships can suffer.

- There's a lost sense of identity and hope.
- People are left to grieve the loss of their former selves.

You can see why roughly 2.1 million people in the world can become addicted to painkillers and dangerous opioids in an attempt to escape both the physical and emotional consequences of a physical condition (or multiple conditions) they can't shake.

Answers as to why they have pain are elusive, as are the solutions, which has created an opening for Big Pharma to come to the rescue. Our sickness and pain are their gain, and business is booming. You need only turn on the TV to witness one of the major drug suppliers touting their latest miracle drug to know how massive the chronic pain business has become. There's a drug for just about every ache, pain, illness, twitch, cough, sneeze, and itch. Of course, the symptoms being treated are usually dwarfed by the potentially disastrous side effects of the drug, like nausea, thoughts of suicide, liver failure, and a potentially fatal infection in the perineum (what?), but big pharma is ready and waiting with a host of other drugs to manage those, too.

Over the last two decades, pharmaceutical revenues worldwide totaled nearly $1.5 trillion. In 2022, the five largest pharmaceutical companies in the US made a combined $81.9 billion. Yet, despite their financial success and the apparent availability of more drugs and medications than one can count, the war on pain rages on.

It isn't that these companies aren't putting out helpful products; countless drugs, vaccines, and medications are literally life savers. However, not everyone is reaping the rewards, and there's a reason it's difficult for many to see a solution to their pain coming anytime soon.

To better understand why, it's crucial to understand the constraints of the current system and why it is failing so many people so that you may know when and how to step outside the box.

As you'll learn—though we are each individually responsible for our health—chronic pain isn't just an individual battle; it's a societal epidemic fueled in part by the very entities we turn to for help.

## Chapter 3

## A FLAWED SYSTEM

PANCHO SEGURA WAS a tennis phenom who became one of the top players in the world in the 1940s and '50s. He was different from other tennis players, though. As a child growing up in Ecuador, he suffered from rickets, a nutritional deficiency that causes the bones in the legs to bow outward. As a result, he didn't walk or run like the other kids, which made it improbable he'd have much success in a game that requires agility and speed.

If he were going to compete successfully, Pancho realized that he would have to change his strategy. Instead of playing like everyone else, he needed at least one shot to get him out of trouble, so he developed a devastating two-handed forehand, later dubbed "the best shot in the game of tennis" by his peers. He also became a master at analyzing his opponent's weaknesses. As a result, he became one of the smartest and craftiest players in the game, eventually landing in the International Tennis Hall of Fame.

When I was a teen trying to rise up the junior tennis ranks, I was lucky to receive some sage advice from Pancho that I'll now pass on to you. He stressed two things that would lead to success:

1. Always know your opponent's strengths and weaknesses so you can develop a proper game plan.
2. Never change a winning strategy, but always change a losing one.

If you're dealing with chronic pain, you've likely been stuck playing the same game as everyone else, and you're slowly descending into the abyss of despair. It's time to heed Pancho's advice and change your strategy. Before you can do that, you need to understand the strengths and weaknesses inherent in the Western medical model of health care.

Modern medicine is undoubtedly a godsend for the vast majority of ailments. Its strengths lie in the ability of extremely knowledgeable doctors, nurses, surgeons, and physical therapists to use proven scientific methodologies and skills to piece us back together when we're broken.

We all know the healthcare system isn't perfect, but for most people, it works. Like a large fishnet that captures all shapes, sizes, and species of fish, most injuries, illnesses, and ailments are brilliantly dealt with and solved.

Yet, despite its successes, the healthcare system has some massive weaknesses, and those in chronic pain are the ones most likely to slip through the holes in the net. It's not the doctors' fault—they're simply doing exactly what they've been trained to do. Instead, it's due to ineffective tools, how our health system is set up, and, at times, a losing strategy.

Here are ten (of many) reasons why the Western model of healthcare falls short for many in pain:

1. Doctors have become individually specialized.
2. The body is treated in pieces and parts.
3. The site of the pain is treated as the cause of the pain.
4. Most healthcare is symptom-driven.
5. Only the physical parts of us are addressed.
6. Many doctors and therapists are stressed for time.
7. Alternative therapies are often construed as inferior.
8. Unnecessary surgeries and treatments are rampant.
9. There's a one-size-fits-all approach.
10. We're conditioned to look outside ourselves for solutions.

## Doctors Are Specialized

Neurosurgeons perform brain surgery, gastroenterologists study the digestive system, and cardiologists treat the heart. Even orthopedists are trained to focus on only one or two joints out of hundreds. There's a specialist for every part of the body, and treatment corresponds to the specialty. If something goes wrong with another system, you see a different doctor who usually prescribes a different medication or treatment.

Unfortunately, one treatment can often contradict the other, as was the case with a woman I worked with who suffered from persistent pain in her lower back. She was prescribed back surgery by the spine specialist, physical therapy and exercise by another specialist, and muscle relaxers by the general practitioner. This is common for people with chronic pain.

The real trouble comes when there are multiple pains or health conditions involved. Take fibromyalgia, for example, which is a condition identified by unexplained pain in numerous areas of the body, constant fatigue, depression, and other symptoms. One of my clients with this condition was taking anti-depression meds prescribed by her psychologist while doing twenty different back, neck, and knee exercises (which were all exhausting her) from her physical therapist. She was also scheduled for wrist surgery with the hand specialist and was working with a gastroenterologist for her stomach issues. Months of her life and thousands of dollars were spent jumping from one physician to the next while hoping for answers and never understanding how and if her symptoms were related. She was a perfect example of how specialization can put some people on a confusing path that winds up, down, and sideways, but ends up right back where they started.

## The Body is Treated in Pieces and Parts

As a result of multiple specialists treating different ailments, many doctors fail to treat the body as a whole, interconnected unit.

Take my client with fibromyalgia. After listening to her story, it wasn't difficult to link all her symptoms together. For example, her back, neck, knee, and wrist pain were all clearly due to severe (but fixable) muscle imbalances that were throwing off her alignment. Her depression was due to the fact that she wasn't making progress and felt powerless to change her situation. She also lived in a constant state of worry and anxiety that she wouldn't ever get better, which explained her fatigue and stomach issues. Not only were they all connected, but they were all solvable without drugs or surgery and without spending five days a week going to specialists. Yet, that's what happens when the strategy is to treat one piece at a time.

By the way, fibromyalgia isn't a disease like cancer or Parkinson's. It's simply a description of symptoms that physicians can't explain. The same is true for chronic fatigue syndrome. They usually don't know how all the symptoms of fatigue and pain are connected. Almost every person I've treated with multiple symptoms had absolutely no idea their issues could be connected until I pointed it out to them. That's because we're taught to treat shoulder pain with shoulder exercises, back pain with back exercises, and neck pain with exercises to stretch and strengthen the neck.

As you'll see in the upcoming chapter on posture, these pains are almost always interconnected. Treating them individually not only misses the obvious connection but can also be ineffective and even detrimental, considering all the unnecessary surgeries and medications given to patients every single day.

For example, I can't tell you how many people have had wrist surgery when the problem could have been solved by realigning their shoulder and upper arm. Unnecessary back and neck surgeries could have been avoided with a few exercises to rebalance and realign the spine.

The point is that doctors aren't trained to treat the body as an interconnected unit; they're trained to address the symptoms.

## The Site of the Pain is Treated as the Cause of the Pain

When pieces and parts are treated without acknowledging how those parts are connected, the message is that the site of the pain is the cause of the pain. For instance, when you visit a doctor for hip pain, they'll take X-rays of your hip. If the X-ray doesn't show anything of diagnostic value, they'll do an MRI. The next step is to send you to a physical therapist or schedule you for surgery. Either way, they're treating the hip—the site of the pain—as if it's the cause of the pain. But how did the hip become damaged to begin with? Why is that hip damaged and not the other? What else is going on in the body that might be connected, like back pain or knee pain?

In the absence of blunt physical trauma like a car accident, getting tackled, or a bad fall, there is another reason for the pain. The MRI or X-ray doesn't tell you how the hip became damaged; it just shows the damage. Similarly, with a herniated or ruptured spinal disc, the what of the damage is clear, but how it became damaged is never treated. Since surgery or therapy only focuses on the site of the pain, the message is clear: the site and the cause are one and the same.

In my experience, that's hardly ever the case. The site of the pain is almost always a symptom of a larger issue. A disc herniates because of imbalanced pressure on one side of the spine, which is always caused by spinal rotation, an imbalance in the function or position of the shoulder blades, and an imbalanced weight distribution in the hips (more on this later).

Hip pain on one side is always due to a misaligned pelvis, which goes hand in hand with an imbalanced and rotated shoulder. In other words, the cause of the pain is *not* the site of the pain. I'm not going to say it never is because absolutes are limiting, but I will say that the vast majority of the time, you need to take in the whole picture if you want to address the root cause.

## The System is Symptom-Driven

Pharmaceutical companies are partly to blame in the sense that every ailment, from stomach pain to arthritis and type 2 diabetes, has a corresponding medication to treat that individual symptom. The message is clear: Take this medication and you'll feel better; there's no need to consider why this happened, and you can continue on with your life. Of course, stomach pain can indicate we're experiencing a great deal of emotional stress, osteoarthritis is nearly always a sign our joints are misaligned, and type 2 diabetes can be a significant warning sign that we're not eating the right foods or exercising enough. None of those external factors are addressed by taking a medication.

But why should we care as long as there's a drug that diminishes the pain? Because plugging one hole doesn't always keep the ship from sinking.

Add that to specialized medicine, which treats the body in pieces and parts and often fails to address the root causes of pain, and you have a symptom-driven model of care. I'm not saying there isn't a need for it; there absolutely is. I'm not even saying don't take the medications. On the contrary, sometimes they're the fastest and most appropriate way to find relief. I am saying that medication or not, it's incumbent on us to look beyond the symptoms and uncover their roots, which means that sometimes we have to treat the body as a unit and look beyond just the physical.

## Only the Physical Parts of Us are Addressed

We are physical beings, but we also have thoughts, feelings, and a spirituality that transcends physicality. There is a mountain of scientific evidence to support the impact of our beliefs and emotions, the power of meditation, past and present trauma, and emotional stress on our health. None of these are addressed when you visit the doctor for back pain, gastrointestinal distress, or even cancer. Therefore, we're putting all our faith in a system that only treats a small part of us.

Doctors can't and shouldn't be expected to address these other aspects of our lives, but we can and should, especially when facing something chronic. Unfortunately, our parents taught us just as their parents taught them that a physical ailment is just that—physical.

Not everyone thinks that way, though. Many cultures still invoke a mind-body-spirit approach to healing. Ayurvedic and Traditional Chinese medicine, for example, began thousands of years ago and are still used to treat billions of people. They're based on the principle that mental and physical well-being are inseparable. Practitioners of both believe that emotions impact the health of the body, and that the body's functions impact a person's emotions.

Even Hippocrates, who started the very first form of modern medicine as we know it, believed that emotions greatly affected the organs and bodily systems. His form of medicine dominated the Western medical approach to healing for over 2000 years. It ended with the invention of the microscope and the discovery of germs and viruses, at which point the mind and body were divided into two separate fields of practice. That was also when our thoughts and emotions ceased to matter, especially when it came to healing. You can't afford to think that way if you're dealing with chronic pain. It's my belief that you have to acknowledge all the parts of you that are hurting even if your health practitioner doesn't.

## Many Doctors and Therapists are Stressed for Time

Short appointment times top the list of patients' most common complaints when visiting their doctors. There's ample evidence to show that their concerns are valid.

A large cross-sectional study of over 4 million patients published in the *Journal of American Medicine* in 2023 showed that the average doctor-and-patient visit appointment time lasted eighteen minutes and that publicly insured patients, as well as Black and Hispanic patients, typically had shorter appointment times compared to others of different backgrounds.

That's disheartening in itself, but it gets worse: The study also reported that shorter appointment times corresponded to a higher likelihood of inappropriate prescriptions of antibiotics and opioids.[1]

To sum that up, in case it wasn't clear, shorter appointment times can mean a higher likelihood of receiving inappropriate treatment, and you're more likely to receive a shorter appointment if you're not White or privately insured.

Patients aren't the only ones complaining. Doctors also want to spend more time with their patients, but it often isn't possible. Diminished reimbursement costs from insurance companies force doctors and physical therapists to see more patients, and new guidelines have increased the amount of paperwork physicians are required to fill out for each patient. The result is that there isn't enough time in the day.

By a recent estimate, primary care doctors would have to spend twenty-seven hours a day to "provide all guideline-recommended preventive, chronic disease, and acute care to a typical patient."[2]

Clearly, short appointment times aren't ideal for anyone.

## Alternative Therapies are Construed as Inferior

From a very young age, we were taught to go directly to the doctor when sick or injured. The message was that doctors are the experts and have all the answers. Many people sincerely believe that if the doctors don't know what's wrong, nobody does. Unfortunately, that severely

---

[1] Neprash HT, Mulcahy JF, Cross DA, Gaugler JE, Golberstein E, Ganguli I. Association of Primary Care Visit Length With Potentially Inappropriate Prescribing. *JAMA Health Forum*. 2023;4(3):e230052. doi:10.1001/jamahealthforum.2023.0052

[2] Porter J, Boyd C, Skandari MR, Laiteerapong N. Revisiting the Time Needed to Provide Adult Primary Care. J Gen Intern Med. 2023 Jan;38(1):147-155. doi: 10.1007/s11606-022-07707-x. Epub 2022 Jul 1. PMID: 35776372; PMCID: PMC9848034.

limits their options and, all too often, their outcomes.

I'm a huge fan of looking elsewhere, especially to "alternative therapies," as they're unfortunately called. Despite the mountains of scientific evidence backing many of them, including postural therapy and meditation, they're often construed as less effective because they aren't part of mainstream medicine.

Let me tell you for a fact, as one of those people in the alternative world, that there are dozens of alternative therapies and healing modalities that can work better for some conditions, especially chronic pain, compared to anything mainstream medicine can offer up.

For example, Cognitive Behavioral Therapy (CBT) has been proven to decrease sensations of pain and increase the quality of life in many people. Meditation has been proven to make the brain less sensitive to pain while increasing the amount of the brain's own pain-reducing opioids. Guided meditation and journaling practices have been shown to improve chronic pain and quality of life.

Numerous studies have shown that massages, acupuncture, nutritional interventions, yoga, and posture therapy can all decrease pain, among other health benefits. So, if you're in pain and haven't ventured into the alternative world, then you're missing out.

The best doctors want you to know that they don't know everything. The more you accept that, the more you can shift your expectations and enjoy the freedom to explore other options that might better serve you.

## Unnecessary Surgeries and Treatments Are Rampant

Have you ever received medical advice that didn't sit well in your gut? Or have you ever felt your doctor didn't know what was causing the pain, yet they recommended tests, medications, or even surgeries you feared weren't necessary?

Have you ever felt like it wasn't your place to question them because, after all, they're the experts?

The truth is, it's called the "practice" of medicine, not the "exactness" of medicine, because that's what they do: they practice medicine. Doctors don't know everything, and they're not always right, so sometimes they have to try many things, hoping to hit the target. Thankfully, they often nail it and save the day, but many times they don't.

A study done in 2017 with 544 patients with back pain revealed that up to 60 percent of surgeries were deemed unnecessary.[3] Multiple other studies on patients with low back pain who underwent surgery concluded that up to 50 percent of lumbar surgeries were unnecessary. Similar studies conducted on patients suffering from knee, neck, and hip pain have also determined a high incidence of surgeries that were neither helpful nor warranted.

There might also be a financial motivation to perform these surgeries. During the COVID pandemic, when hospitals hit the pause button on surgeries that were deemed elective, US health centers suffered up to a 42 percent drop in revenue. Specifically, it was found that a decrease in hip and knee replacement surgeries played a large role. The statistics show that typical US hospitals rely heavily on revenue from non-emergency procedures like joint and spine surgeries and struggle to stay afloat when relying solely on patients who require immediate in-person care. This clearly highlights the amount of pressure on physicians to perform surgeries that may not be necessary in order to stay profitable.

To avoid an unnecessary procedure to the best of your ability, I recommend four things:

1. Never be afraid to ask questions or to challenge a diagnosis.

2. Always get a second opinion when surgery is on the table (doctors disagree with each other up to 60 percent of the time in some instances).

---

3 Lenza M, Buchbinder R, Staples MP, Dos Santos OFP, Brandt RA, Lottenberg CL, Cendoroglo M, Ferretti M. Second opinion for degenerative spinal conditions: an option or a necessity? A prospective observational study. BMC Musculoskelet Disord. 2017 Aug 17;18(1):354. doi: 10.1186/s12891-017-1712-0. PMID: 28818047; PMCID:

3. Give your instincts plenty of proper consideration.
4. Never be afraid to seek out alternative options, especially when there's little downside if they fail.

## Too Often There's a One-Size-Fits-All Approach

What all doctors and physical therapists know but won't tell you is that most pain, including back pain, resolves itself without intervention 75 percent of the time. So, what happens the rest of the time? Patients end up doing unnecessary surgeries or going to physical therapy only to do the same stretching and strengthening exercises that everyone else with the same pain who has come before them and will come after them will receive.

After working with thousands of people in pain, I can tell you that no two people and no two bodies are exactly alike. To use back pain as an example, the pain in my back was related to extreme emotional distress related to athletic and parental pressure, added to a very tight mid-back. Your back pain might be related to tight hip flexors and abdominals, hips that are misaligned, and stress around work. Certainly, no matter what condition you're dealing with, it helps to tease some of these things out so that appropriate treatment can follow, but that's not the norm. As a result, too many people with chronic pain are given the cookie-cutter approach to treatment and therapy, and it doesn't work. Everybody, and every body, is unique, and an approach that can acknowledge and accommodate that fact is essential when other methods fail.

## We're Conditioned to Look Outside Ourselves

When was the last time you were sick or injured, and in addition to soliciting advice from a physician, you looked inward at your stress levels, actually meditated, and asked yourself how the painful condition might relate to your thoughts and emotions? I'm guessing that for most, the answer is never.

We're conditioned to run for the quick fix, and we usually find it. Yet, as you'll learn in the upcoming chapters, to take full responsibility for your health, and in the face of an ailment that your body isn't healing, sometimes it helps to acknowledge your thoughts, feelings, beliefs, actions, emotional states, stress levels, and life's ups and downs.

We were never taught that some health challenges can be solved by looking inward rather than spending countless hours and precious financial resources on advice and traditional treatments. We were never taught that we could learn to be the experts on our bodies and that some things can be solved by consulting the wisdom inside ourselves.

Instead, we were taught to rely on someone else to make us healthy. Yet, when we delegate our health to someone else, we leave it entirely up to their experience and judgment. Being human, they aren't always right. I'm a huge believer in listening to our instincts and learning how to decipher our bodies' messages. That way, we can work with our physicians and health practitioners to find the best solutions to our health concerns.

Of course, these are just some of the reasons the healthcare system fails so many in chronic pain. There are others, including insurance companies' unwillingness to pay for many alternative treatments and the overall high cost of healthcare. According to the United States Pain Foundation, people with severe pain spend an average of $644 per month ($7,726 per year) more on expenses for annual health care than people without severe pain.

There's also a barrage of disinformation (fake news, in modern lingo) about what causes chronic pain. In fact, there are a great number of false idols that have gone uncontested for far too long. It's time to change that, but before we examine some of them, let me warn you that you're probably not in pain for the reason you think or have been told.

## Chapter 4

## WHAT DOESN'T CAUSE CHRONIC PAIN

THERE ISN'T A one-size-fits-all answer to what causes chronic pain, but I can tell you generally what doesn't. Culturally, we've come to accept some common convictions about pain, many of which can be misleading, disempowering, and even flat-out wrong. On the surface, they might sound like reasonable explanations, but when you examine them further, you'll see the holes and realize they lack one crucial ingredient: common sense.

Unfortunately, these myths are innocently and unwittingly propagated by health practitioners every single day. Myths about the causes of chronic pain are so rampant that you'll find yourself wondering how they can be myths at all. I assure you, though, they're often just as false as the earth being flat and cigarette smoking being good for you.

### Myth #1: Pain is Purely Physical

I touched on this in the last chapter regarding the flaws of modern medicine, but it's worth investigating a little further because it's one of the most detrimental myths in our society. The irony is that the medical system already knows pain isn't just physical. How do I know?

Because every single drug that every pharmaceutical company makes is compared to a placebo before it can be approved. A placebo is a sugar pill that is supposed to have absolutely no biochemical altering or healing properties. Yet, people respond to it up to 30 percent of the time, and sometimes more.

How can that be? The answer is the power of belief, and the FDA doesn't approve drugs if they don't beat the power of belief, more commonly referred to as the placebo effect. Therefore, pharmaceutical companies routinely harness that power to make a drug more effective. For instance, studies have shown that the color, shape, taste, and even the name of a tablet or pill can improve the pill's efficacy and even reduce the pill's side effects. Further, red, yellow, and orange pills are associated with a stimulant effect, while blue and green colors are associated with a tranquilizing effect. Even the name of a drug is carefully selected because it's been shown to either enhance or diminish the patient's perceptions (and thus the outcome) of its potency.

The lesson is that there's more to healing than the biochemical effectiveness of a medication. There are other things inside us impacting our biology every day. What are they? They're our thoughts, emotions, perceptions, and beliefs. As I pointed out in the last chapter, we are physical, but we are also thought and emotional and spiritual energy. If you're thinking, feeling, or believing that you're broken or that something out of your control is causing your pain, it can be impeding your ability to heal. Instead of acting as a placebo, which often impacts people's health positively, detrimental beliefs can act as noceboes, which can affect you and your health negatively.

That's why I'd like to dispel some other myths or things you might have been told about the causes of chronic pain. I hope this new knowledge will alter your perceptions so that you can shift some of your beliefs and adopt new ones that serve you better.

## Myth #2: It's All in Your Head

Your pain might result from many different influences, but one thing's for sure: it isn't all in your head. Pete Egoscue, one of my mentors and a pioneer of postural therapy, started his journey to solve musculoskeletal pain because a doctor diagnosed that the pain shooting down his leg was purely psychological. He's one of many I've encountered over the years who have been told the same.

How does one become the unfortunate recipient of such unhelpful advice? If the pain can't be explained via an apparent cause, or if it fails to respond to traditional treatment, many physicians will throw their hands up in bewilderment. Some will conclude that the pain must be psychological, leaving many people feeling like they're all alone, irreparably broken, and apparently crazy.

Psychogenic, psychosomatic, neurogenic, and any other term used to describe pain that emanates from a psychological, emotional, or neurological origin doesn't indicate that the pain is imaginary or made up. It means the pain is very real; it's just not coming from the pain sensors located outside your central nervous system. This is good news, because it indicates that you're not broken. Doctors are ill-equipped to deal with this kind of pain, but that doesn't mean you can't solve it. At the very least, you can be assured of one thing: You aren't crazy.

## MYTH #3: IT'S YOUR GENETICS

In my previous book, *Ageless, Painless Tennis*, I told the story of a twenty-five-year-old woman who came to me on crutches complaining of pain in her ankle. The doctors told her she'd likely never run again lest she do severe damage to the joint. When I asked her what she thought was causing her pain, she said, "My doctors say it's severe tendonitis." I replied, "What do you think it is?" She thought momentarily before replying, "My dad had tennis elbow" (cue ten seconds of uncomfortable silence as I waited for more explanation). I was as confused as you likely are about this statement until I finally relented and asked her to explain. "Well, my dad must have passed on weak tendons and ligaments." Ah ha! She was playing the genetics card.

I asked her to drop the crutches, put her hands behind her head, interlace her fingers, pull her elbows back, and walk for me. If you need to imagine this position, think of Bruce Willis at the end of *Die Hard*, with his hands behind his head and the gun taped behind his back right before he saved the day. Anyway, after assuming the position, she walked with no pain. The short answer to why that worked is that it changed her alignment, not her genes.

We blame pain and disease on many things, few of which are actually the cause. Our genes are a perfect example.

In his book *The Biology of Belief*, Dr. Bruce Lipton remarks: "Less than one percent of disease is associated with genetics. Over 90 percent of disease is a total reflection of the environment and especially our programming: the disempowering, self-sabotaging behaviors we acquired in the first seven years. Since those disempowering programs are based on our environment and our perception, and since we can change the environment and our perception, we have the power to free ourselves from disease and to start living that happily-ever-after honeymoon of life experiences that we all believe that we can have."

I'm with Dr. Lipton. In my experience, even if your parents passed on a few spades, that doesn't mean nothing can be done. Like the woman I just described, it certainly doesn't mean that genetics are causing your pain. In fact, I can almost guarantee that it isn't genetics. Your belief that it is might be, though.

I once had another client with pain in her right knee who claimed it was passed on from her mother, who had bad knees. I jokingly pointed out that her left knee, the "good knee," must have come from her father.

I've got all kinds of one-liners to counter shaky beliefs about pain, but here's a line and a new belief you can adapt that's backed by science: Just because you have a gene doesn't mean it will be expressed, and it certainly doesn't mean you're doomed.

Epigeneticists are learning that the most significant factor in whether good or bad genes are turned on or off depends on our environment, not the genes themselves. The environment is that of our thoughts, emotional states, and stress levels. There's also the effect of unhealed past traumatic experiences that impacts all three.

Besser van der Kolk writes in his book, *The Body Keeps the Score*, "Trauma survivors are vulnerable to a host of medical illnesses and chronic pain syndromes, insomnia, drug and alcohol addiction, depression, obesity, and other issues related to optimal functioning of the entire organism, and the capacity for self-regulation and self-care."

The conclusion is that if you want to heal, let go of your hold on the genetics card and focus instead on healing some of the hurt, abandonment, and anger from your past while shifting your thoughts and beliefs toward something more empowering, like "I can heal, I will heal, and I have the genes inside me to make it happen."

## Myth #4: It's Your Age

Many people anticipate that growing older means growing weaker, more fragile, and increasingly feeble with every passing year, especially after the age of [fill in your number here for when you think you will have turned the corner from young and invincible to old and frail].

I'll never forget the time a few years ago when I was playing singles against a kid fresh off his college tennis team. As his frustration was building, I hit an ace, to which he proclaimed in pure annoyance, "I just got aced by my grandfather!" I broke out laughing, first because I could really only be his father, and second, because it clearly showed his belief that you can't be a good athlete after a certain age, not to mention after the hopelessly ancient age of forty-five!

The good news is that our energy levels, physical ability, strength, weight, conditioning, and youthfulness don't correspond to our birthdays.

In her book *Breaking the Age Code*, Becca Levy documents a study she conducted on the impact of cultural age stereotypes on the health and lives of older people. The results were telling.

She found that "older people with more positive perceptions of aging performed better physically and cognitively." Specifically, she found that they were more likely to recover from severe disability, they walked faster, had better memories, and lived longer than those with negative perceptions of aging. Levy was also able to show that hearing loss, cardiovascular disease, dementia, and even Alzheimer's were also "the products of age beliefs absorbed from our social surroundings." Her findings support that certain unhelpful beliefs can significantly impact our short and long-term health.

I can't tell you how many people I've worked with who believe their pain or disability is due to getting older. That's why I habitually ask my clients why they think they have pain, especially on one side of the body, like in one knee or shoulder.

My favorite answer is when they say, "I think I'm just getting older." I ask how old the other shoulder is, then watch them smile as the silliness of their answer sinks in.

It doesn't end with ankles, shoulders, and knees, though. Bad backs, arthritis, muscle strains, neck pain, migraines, digestive issues, and the like are often all piled up together like dirty laundry, thrown into the age hamper, and washed with shaky reasoning, bad advice, and limited beliefs, then come out the other side as smelly as they were when they went in.

Age is never a good reason for pain. First of all, that belief makes you a victim of aging, which means you're powerless to fix it. Second, in my experience, it's never true. Yes, we all undergo age-related changes like graying hair and skin wrinkles. Still, joint pain and frailty don't have to be part of the package as long as you're limiting the amount of postural and emotional stress, remaining active, staying engaged in your community, hanging out often with a group of close-knit friends, and continuing to stay curious about yourself and your world (all of which are scientifically proven factors in longevity and happiness).

It doesn't mean that pain will never find you; the science says there will likely be much less frequent and shorter bouts of it, similar to what we all experience at every age.

Whatever your expectations or beliefs, it is a biological and anatomical fact that we can gain strength, fitness, energy, flexibility, and the right emotional state at just about any age short of too late, and injuries and illness don't have to correspond to getting older.

A belief that they do will undoubtedly increase the likelihood that they'll occur, though, so be very clear on what's true and what isn't when it comes to any beliefs you have about your pain and aging.

## Myth #5: It's a Lack of Core Strength

I bet if you're dealing with chronic back pain or any other muscle or joint ailment, including arthritis, you've been told you need more core strength. In fact, I can hear you protesting this very moment: "David, core strength is vital to staying healthy." That all depends on what you call core strength.

Let me tell you where the idea of core strength as a remedy for musculoskeletal pain began and how it became the purported cure-all for everything short of, well, being too short.

The idea of core strength as a solution for back pain began when researchers in Australia discovered that specific stomach muscles, particularly the transverse abdominis, contract to stabilize the spine before we make any movement. You can test this now by bringing your attention to your stomach muscles and then reaching forward to pick up a book. You'll notice that your stomach muscles will engage right before you lift the book. This is your body's natural and unconscious bracing and spinal stabilizing mechanism in action. Those same Australian researchers found that the people in their study with back pain weren't contracting their transverse abdominis, so they correlated that muscle not working with the pain.

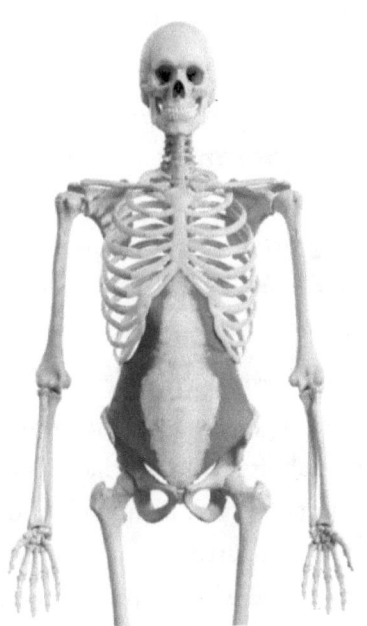

*The Transverse Abdominis*

Unfortunately, some health practitioners and others in the public took that information and made their own conclusions, specifically that all weak stomach muscles meant back pain. Now, it's commonplace to be told to strengthen your abs at all costs. I was one of the recipients of that often-unhelpful advice.

Since that Australian study, several other studies have shown that people can have back pain regardless of the strength of their transverse abdominis, which was definitely true in my case. Unfortunately, though, the cat was out of the bag, and core strengthening became all the rage, not to mention the purported "cure for back pain."

Now, here's an excerpt from Wikipedia citing different studies on core strength:

> *"Evidence published . . . has found no significant difference between core stability exercises and general exercises with respect to low back pain in the short term or long term, even though both interventions did improve pain and function temporarily."*

Let me give you another conclusion about sports performance from a different set of studies:

> *"There is little support in research for the core stability model, and many of the benefits attributed to this method of exercise have not been demonstrated. At best, core stability training has the same benefits as general, non-specific exercise. Trunk or core-specific exercise have failed to demonstrate preventative benefits against injuries in sports or to improve sports performance."*

So, to sum up, numerous scientific studies have shown that transverse abdominis strength does not necessarily correlate to low back pain, and core stability exercises have been proven to have minimal long-term effects on back pain while showing no difference in improving pain levels compared to general exercise.

Are you beginning to see why, despite all the core strengthening devices, exercises, and advice in the world, there is still a global low back pain epidemic? I'm very sorry to tell you the advice you've been getting, and the advice the "health experts" have been peddling about strengthening your core, has been misleading at best and flat-out wrong for many people in pain. I can personally attest to this not only as someone who has worked with countless people with back pain, but as someone who could do a hundred sit-ups in a minute and still had back pain every day for years.

Can traditional core strengthening help some people? Yes, but I believe it has more to do with the fact that any exercise routine that provides the body with new, varied stimulus and motion helps most people, not because it's specific to the core. Plus, throwing a bunch of core-strengthening exercises at someone indicates the real cause is still likely misunderstood. It could be tight hip flexors, a kyphotic upper back, emotional distress adding to both, and more—none of which are addressed with drugs, surgery, and any exercise that purportedly strengthens the core. Don't get me wrong; there can be a time and place for it, but it's important to understand the cause of the pain first and then agree on exactly what core strength is really about.

Traditionally, beyond the transverse abdominis, health experts have thought of the core as all the abdominals, the glutes, the muscles that line the spine, the diaphragm, and even the pelvic floor muscles. These muscles all work in conjunction to provide stability to the spine. However, when the alignment of your shoulders, hips, and spine is off, those muscles and all the others that work to stabilize all the joints in the body can't work together anymore. Some stabilizing muscles are turned off altogether, or their activation is turned way down. That includes two of the most important stabilizers of your spine, the psoas and the diaphragm, both of which work to provide tension, stability, and balance between the front and back sides of the body, which is crucial when it comes to keeping the muscles and structures of the spine happy and healthy.

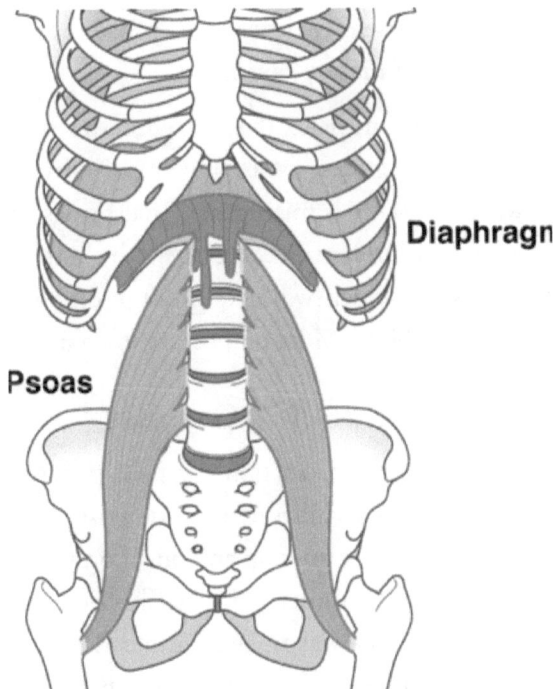

*The diaphragm is pictured underneath the rib cage, while the psoas attaches directly to the spinal vertebrae. Both help to stabilize the spine.*

The problem is, in most people, the diaphragm is often shut down or working at half capacity. There are two reasons for this:

1. Most people hold constant tension in their abdominals due to emotional stress, like worry, fear, anxiety, and other emotions they're trying to keep at bay. The result is that people take over 20,000 breaths a day entirely from their upper chest rather than from the diaphragm, which changes the diaphragm's ability to create intra-abdominal pressure and, therefore, spinal stability.

2. Most people have postural imbalances, like too much rounding in their shoulders and upper back, and their hips are out of alignment. These postural imbalances change the tension on the scapular stabilizers, the psoas, and the spine, creating an environment where neither the psoas nor the diaphragm can function optimally.

So, to sum up, the muscles that stabilize the spine, like the diaphragm, abdominals, glutes, psoas, and spinal musculature, can't do their jobs when the body is misaligned. That brings us right back to posture. Improve your postural alignment by restoring balance to your body's muscles, which will take pressure off your spine and improve your spinal stability. More on posture to come.

## Myth #6: It's Overuse

Overuse is a common explanation for pain. Knee pain, carpal tunnel, arthritis, back pain, Achilles tendonitis, wrist pain—the list of ailments attributed to overuse goes on and on. If only it made sense.

A man came to me with knee pain that his doctors concluded was from overuse because he was an avid runner. They reasoned that running is hard on the knees (it's actually been shown to strengthen the joint and make it more resilient to stress), and because of his age (ahem) and overuse, his knee was finally talking to him. I asked him if he had been running on both legs, or if he had only been running on just the overused one all these years. He said he likes to run on both legs. (I told you not to mess with me when it comes to shaky pain reasoning).

It doesn't matter what muscle, joint, or area of the body is in pain. It's never an overuse problem. There is such a thing as underuse, because the joint can weaken, but the overuse explanation often indicates there was a failure to explore the issue at a deeper level. Again, it's not the health practitioner's fault; this is how we've all been taught to look at the body and to explain a condition we may not fully understand.

If you're still unsure whether it's overuse or not, answer these questions: If it's an overuse problem, why is the part suddenly hurting after all these months or years? How long have you been doing the activity (typing, running, walking, swimming) that's causing the overuse? Why isn't the other side hurting despite performing the same activity?

If you can't come up with any solid answers, I invite you to discard the undercooked, overused "overuse" explanation.

Now, there is one caveat. There is such a thing as overuse and out of position. That means the back, knee, wrist, or shoulder joint is out of alignment, and it can only handle so many reps using muscles, joints, tendons, and ligaments that aren't designed to do that job. The misalignment is the ultimate cause, but enough reps in this disadvantaged position will make any joint or muscle begin to complain.

Carpal tunnel syndrome is a perfect example. No, it isn't due to typing at a computer all day. It is due to typing at a computer with your shoulders rounded forward, your arm bones rotated in and disconnected from your lower arm and wrist for months or years. That's when the muscles and tendons of the wrist become isolated and do a job they're not meant to do alone. Usually, even then, it takes another stress added on top of the misalignment to kick off the pain, whether it's a fall on your shoulder, lifting weights, strength training, or some emotional turmoil that pushes the body and brain over the edge.

The solution is to realign the arm bones and the upper back, let the body heal, address the emotional stress, and then go back to typing without pain.

## Myth #7: You Overdid It

Oh, really? Again, I have questions: How many times did the other side of your body do the same action? How many times have you done that activity or movement in the past without a problem?

If overdoing it was the culprit, then you're either very deconditioned, or you ran an ultra-marathon and actually did overdo it. Even then, I'm skeptical, because why did your body break at that exact point? Why that knee or side of your back and not the other?

It's much more likely you're experiencing the same thing as everyone else who overused their body in some way—postural and emotional stress, which we'll explore in the upcoming chapters.

Here's another question: I assume you're not overdoing it anymore, so why hasn't your body healed?

The answer goes back to what I mentioned in the first chapter. If you're not healing despite being a magical healing machine, something is blocking your body's ability to heal, and you need to uncover what that is.

So, without further ado, let's dive into the journal questions that follow to explore your beliefs. Are they placebos that are serving you, or noceboes that are sabotaging you? The idea is to uncover more than a few unhelpful beliefs influencing your life and body more profoundly than you may know.

I call it the "Healing Journal," because these questions and others in the following chapters are designed to help you go under the surface and connect to yourself, your beliefs, or your emotions so that you may clear away any obstacles and kickstart your body's healing superpower.

# Healing Journal

As impressionable, highly aware beings hell-bent on attempting to make sense of ourselves and the world around us, we tend to form deeply embedded beliefs about our health and how we should live our lives. We developed these beliefs over time, usually due to unconscious conditioning downloaded into our brains during our first thirty years of life.

Part of our unconscious and conscious conditioning was born from carefully watching our elders and taking note of everything about them, including their attitudes, their beliefs, how they walk, how they talk, what foods they ingest, their injuries, aches, and pains, and even when they die.

Whatever beliefs we've incorporated into our lives and bodies, we must take full responsibility for them. If we blame anyone or anything for our suffering or pain, we're giving away our power and ability to achieve the optimal health and happiness we deserve. Take some time to answer these questions on a piece of paper or in your journal. They may give you some insight into why you've been struggling. The answers might also help you clear the way for your body to heal.

1. What have you been told or led to believe about your health condition? Is it due to age, poor genetics, overuse, lousy luck, overdoing it, a lack of core strength, or something else?

2. Why do you believe you're in pain and haven't been able to heal? (Pay close attention to whether you're blaming someone or something out of your control.

3. Who were your models of health growing up, and what health challenges did they face?

4. What beliefs about health, healing, and pain have they passed on to you?

5. Has your health or your life mirrored those of your parents or caregivers?

6. If so, do you think you can change your fate, or are their health challenges destined to be yours?

7. Do you believe you're destined for a painful or debilitating health condition in the future? If so, what can you do now to change the outcome? It's becoming common to see more and more models of health, curiosity, and passion in people of very advanced age. I believe that one day, living well above a hundred will become the new norm, because more and more people will reach it seamlessly and without significant health complications along the way.

8. At what age do you see yourself becoming old and frail?

9. When you close your eyes and picture yourself at seventy years old, are you full of energy, or are you worn out and napping in a lounge chair, waiting to die? Are you weak or strong? Thin or overweight? Are you healthy or taking twenty different medications to stay alive? How about at eighty or ninety? Please take the time to sit with the pictures of your older self in your head. Your thoughts, beliefs, and expectations are working right now to create your future. I bet when you were twenty, forty seemed like an eternity away, and it sounded old. Yet, many

people hit forty and feel no different than when they were twenty, while others reach that age and feel old beyond their years. The same is true for fifty, sixty, and a hundred.

Your future is not written. You can create a new, much healthier, and empowered future simply by examining some of your beliefs about aging, genetics, and health and rewiring your brain to form much more positive outcomes. Choose the beliefs you want to adopt, like the one that you'll be healthy, strong, and pain-free until the end of your very long and fulfilling life.

What new beliefs about healing, aging, or genetics do you want to adopt that will serve you better now and in the future? Write them down in detail so you can create a map of the future you want to create.

Hopefully, you've teased out some of your limiting beliefs and expectations. If not, stop reading, grab some paper or your journal, and answer the questions. I promise you'll be surprised at what comes up if you let down your guard and explore what's inside. Keep in mind that you can't have a choice about the fate of your health if you don't even know what you're choosing, which is why it's critical to bring your beliefs and expectations to the forefront of your awareness.

Now that you have a handle on some things that are generally *not* responsible for chronic pain, it's time to examine a few things that are, starting with postural stress.

# Part II
*Discovering Your Design and the Origins of Pain*

## Chapter 5

# STAND UP STRAIGHT!

JACK COULD BARELY walk. As he hobbled into the room, leaning on one crutch to relieve the weight off of his aching, arthritic right knee, he said he needed a miracle. I learned that Jack was an ex-Marine who had seen some severe combat during multiple wars and tours abroad. Remarkably, he'd never been injured during battle, but the physical and emotional strain had taken its toll. He was only fifty-five, but his stiff, painful body reflected that of a much older man who hadn't been allowed to relax for more than a minute in decades.

His right knee was twice the size of his left, which is typical for a severely arthritic joint that's bone-on-bone and lacks the necessary cartilage required to absorb the stress of walking.

His knee wasn't my biggest concern, though; it was merely a symptom of a much larger issue. I was pretty sure he was headed for a total knee replacement, no matter what. My biggest concern was helping him save the rest of his body and his mind so he could live out the next thirty or forty years free of pain, ideally without having to undergo replacement surgeries in both his hips, not to mention spinal surgery to fuse his lower back—all of which looked about as frozen as his knee.

To do that, I explained that two things needed to happen: We would have to address his significant postural and mechanical imbalances, which were the real reasons his right knee wore out—the same imbalances that were putting too much stress on his remaining joints. We also needed to teach his brain to find its way out of fight-or-flight mode, which was keeping his body from relaxing and his mind from finding any semblance of peace.

Jack was all in. After about ninety minutes of specific exercises to realign his body and a relaxing meditation to calm his mind, he walked out without his crutch, feeling like a weight had been lifted off his whole body.

He eventually had the knee replacement, but not before reducing his knee pain by 70 percent with just the exercises alone. Now, he says he hikes every day with his wife and two dogs, and he's truly enjoying his life in a way he was never able to before.

Jack's particular pain may have been unique to him, but the cause of his pain wasn't. Every single person I've worked with over the last several decades who has suffered from chronic pain has had at least two things in common that tipped them over the edge and into pain:

1. Significant postural imbalances, which we'll call "postural stress"
2. Past or present emotional stress (suppressed or not)

Before we discuss the emotional component, I want to give you a thorough understanding of postural stress. Everyone has it to some degree after a certain age, and it can be a very misunderstood concept.

I first learned about posture from Pete Egoscue, who started a postural therapy clinic in the late 1980s and became a leader in posture and musculoskeletal pain. Pete, as he prefers to be called, is a former Marine who was wounded in the Vietnam War. His injuries later led to him developing the Egoscue Method, which is a powerful form of postural therapy in the right hands. His book *Pain Free* states, "When the body is properly aligned, the stress on our joints, bones, and muscles is minimized. When the body falls out of alignment, our joints, bones, and muscles become subject to abnormal stress and strain, increasing our likelihood of injury and pain."

It's that simple: misalignment incurs strain on muscles, bones, and joints, while good alignment doesn't. But what is good posture? It turns out it has nothing to do with your mother's admonishment to stand up straight. Good posture means three things:

1. Your major weight-bearing joints line up under gravity.
2. There is equal muscle tension between the right and left sides of your body as well as the front and back sides.
3. You're able to move through your day, play sports, and enjoy everyday activities without pain, limitation, or injury.

By weight-bearing joints, I mean the large joints simultaneously bearing your body's weight while holding you upright. These are your shoulder, hip, knee, and ankle joints. According to the book *Muscles Testing and Function with Posture and Pain* by Florence Peterson Kendall and others, which was one of the first books to describe posture in great detail, the line of gravity should bisect all the joints but the ankle (the line sits slightly in front), which means the force of gravity is distributed equally throughout each joint and then flows directly through the arch of the foot.

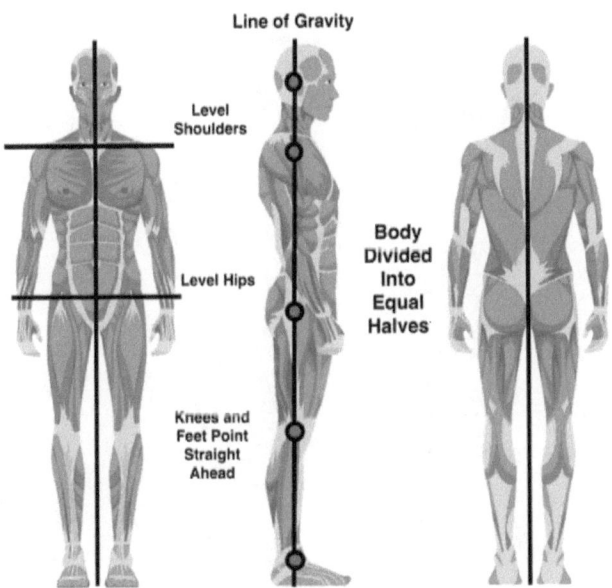

*Gravity is ideally distributed through the middle of the shoulder, hip, and knee joints and just forward of the ankle joint.*

Physics has even more to say about how our bodies are naturally aligned. Under ideal posture, almost no muscle activation is required to maintain a standing position. Even where the force vectors don't travel directly through the bone, the fascia and ligaments surrounding each joint provide ample support to maintain stability. Therefore, any chronic muscle tension in the body is a sign that the joints are misaligned and that those muscles are compensating.

When aligned, the muscles surrounding and attaching to the bones and joints should all be under equal and balanced tension. For example, the back muscles, which bend the spine backward, should be under the same tension as the abdominals, which bend the spine forward. The thigh muscles on the front of the leg, which straighten the knee, should be balanced with the hamstrings on the back of the leg, which bend the knee. Muscles on all sides also work together to produce maximum stability, shock absorption, shock distribution, and full joint motion.

How many people have ideal posture? Not many, but there are some. We call them children.

*All the joints are aligned.*

*The beginning of an unhelpful habit.*

Most kids have ideal posture from the time they first begin to walk to when they start sitting too long for school. Constantly reinforcing forward head posture (text neck) doesn't help either. Some adults are well-aligned, but it's far from the norm these days. Most people have at least some postural imbalances, and many have significant ones.

Why should we care? There are at least six potentially serious consequences of misalignment, all of which can lead to acute or chronic pain:

1. Altered joint function and mechanics
2. Over-strain on specific muscles, tendons, ligaments, fascia, bones and joints
3. Compensation
4. The forming of new, dysfunctional movement patterns and neural pathways

5. Increased predisposition to injury
6. Prevention of proper healing or healing in general

Let me give you an example using the shoulder that highlights all these consequences at once. The shoulder joint is designed to move in all planes and directions, allowing our arms and hands the freedom to reach, push, pull, grab, carry, throw a ball, and do all the things we might do daily. It's our most flexible major joint, while remaining miraculously stable.

Imagine one shoulder has dropped forward and down out of its neutral and anatomically designed position.

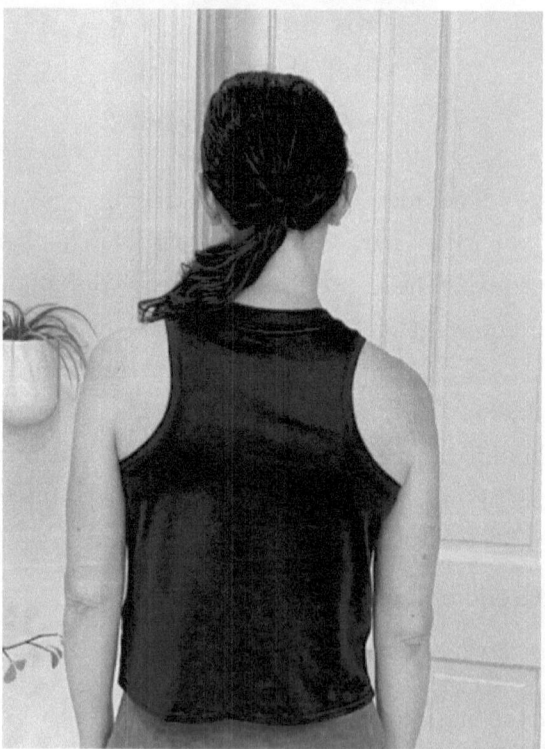

*The right shoulder has dropped down, and the right elbow has rotated forward.*

This is a widespread occurrence for various reasons, which I'll discuss shortly. In this misaligned position, the upper arm bone, shoulder blade, and collar bone can no longer produce smooth, uninhibited motion. Instead, the shoulder blade doesn't glide correctly along the rib cage, the arm bone can't rotate appropriately as it moves, and the collar bone no longer rotates in conjunction with the arm.

You can feel this yourself right now. Sit or stand up straight and raise your right arm overhead as high as possible. Register how high you can raise it. Now, round your shoulders forward like you're slouching and hold that position while you raise your right hand overhead again. Notice that you can't raise your arm nearly as high.

*The position of the shoulders and upper back changes the shoulder's range of motion.*

That's because changing your shoulder's position impacts your shoulder's range of motion (aka function). Every single joint in your body operates this way.

## Positional Change of Any Joint Equals Functional and Mechanical Change of the Joint

That isn't all. If the shoulder function is limited enough, even the rib cage and the upper spine muscles will be impeded from moving through their full range of motion.

Muscles that don't move become tight. When one or both shoulders are rounded forward and remain that way for days, months, or years, some muscles become chronically shortened, while others remain stuck in a lengthened position.

A muscle that's too short can become tight and restrictive, while muscles stretched too long can become ineffective movers and stabilizers. That could be a problem if you're reaching above your head into a cupboard for a glass, trying to undo your bra, going for an overhead smash in pickleball, typing at a computer all day, or doing anything that requires the shoulder to push, pull, and move through a full range of motion.

Log this into your permanent memory bank: *Any* alteration in joint position—and therefore, joint mechanics from neutral and fully functional—predisposes the joint to injury. That doesn't mean it will be injured, but it does mean the likelihood increases proportionally to the amount of positional change and the amount of demand placed on it. In simple terms, if you're trying to serve a ball in tennis, reach in the backseat of your car to grab your sweater, or do any of the activities just mentioned, and your shoulder is out of alignment, you're more likely to injure that shoulder.

Here's an easy chart to understand the effects of misalignment in your shoulders, elbows, wrists, hands, neck, lower back, hips, knees, ankles, and feet:

> *Muscle tension change –> change in joint position –> altered joint range of motion/mechanics –> stress and strain on muscles, tendons, ligaments, joint cartilage –> injury*

There's something else you need to know. When any major

load-bearing joint—shoulder, hip, knee, or ankle—is out of alignment, every joint above and below it is compromised to some degree. How is this possible?

There are at least three ways every joint is connected to every other joint. One connection is via the muscles. For example, a misaligned shoulder creates imbalanced tension on one side of the neck, throughout the muscles of the rib cage, and in all the muscles that move and stabilize the spine.

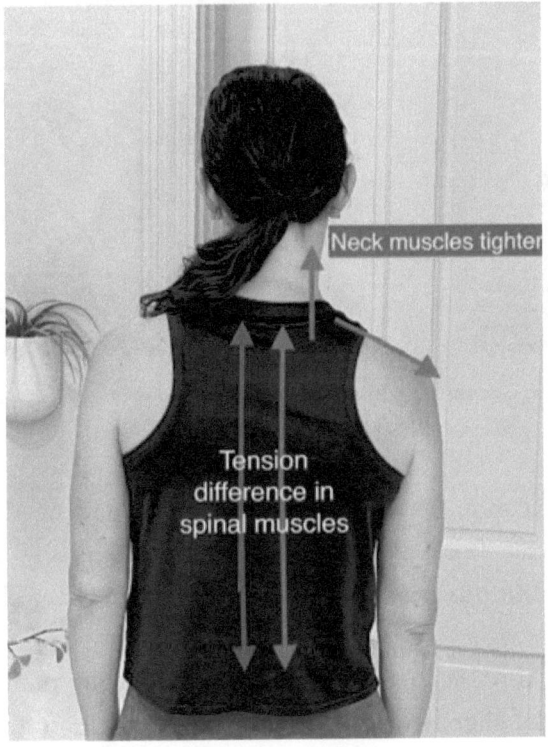

*When a shoulder drops, it changes the tension throughout the spine.*

Those muscles connect to the muscles of the pelvis and the hips, leading to imbalances in those areas. Many of the hip muscles also connect to the knee joint, which has muscle connections with the ankle and the foot.

As you can see, there's a domino-like effect on the muscles in the body, but there's also a fascial connection. Fascia is the connective tissue surrounding and supporting every muscle, organ, bone, blood vessel, nerve fiber, and joint. Imagine a dense network of intertwining spider webs throughout the entire body, and that's your fascia.

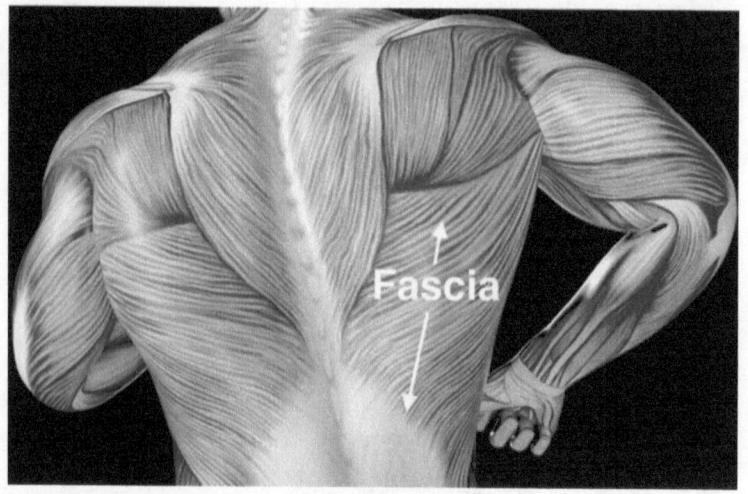

*Fascia is connective tissue seen as the white striations between the muscle fibers.*

You can't move any joint out of position and not impact the tension in your fascia any more than you can ping any strand of a spider web and not alert the spider, even if it's on the other side of the web.

There's also the nervous system. When your brain senses a joint is out of alignment, it instructs other muscles to take over to compensate for those that can no longer maintain adequate stability or motion. Tension changes in those muscles lead to tension changes in the muscles above and below them, and so on. You can't even turn your foot without affecting your neck. You can also discover this by turning your right foot outward about forty-five degrees. Notice, as you turn your right foot out, your left hip has to rotate forward, which takes your left shoulder and knee with it. To continue looking straight ahead, your neck stays still but is now twisted opposite of your upper body.

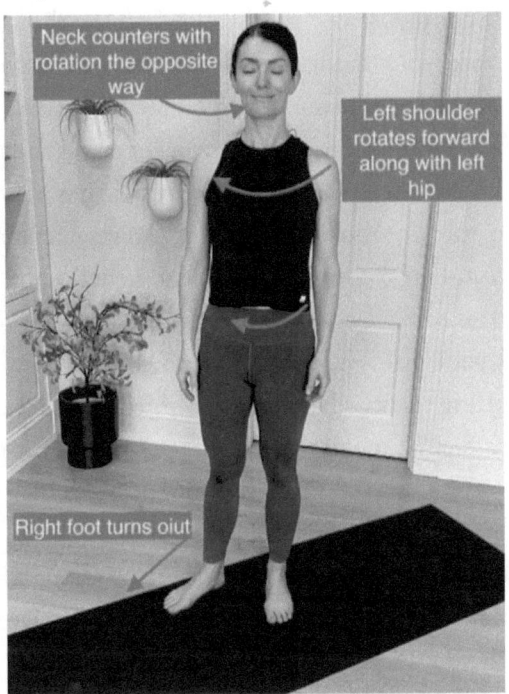

*Consequences of imbalance*

In my experience, this is a typical postural imbalance in seven out of ten people.

It's a common example of a chain reaction from the misalignment of one joint and the resulting postural stress on all the other joints, including the opposite knee.

As you can imagine, pain or injury can happen anywhere in the chain. It can be a torn labrum or rotator cuff in the shoulder that rotated forward, neck pain or a cervical disc herniation, a strained oblique, or one-sided lower back pain. It can also arise as hip pain on either side, pain inside the knee, a torn meniscus, or foot and ankle pain.

Now that you understand how the body is connected as one

interdependent unit, you can begin to trace an injury to its root cause rather than focusing on the symptom as the reason for the pain.

Here's an example of how that works, keeping the same scenario. Imagine you tore your medial meniscus (the cartilaginous cushion between the bones in your knee) while playing tennis. Most people would attribute the injury to a move you made on the tennis court, but that's only *what* you did to tear it, which has very little to do with *why* you tore it. You didn't tear it because tennis is hard on your knee, because of overuse, old age, bad genetics, or even a lousy tennis move. You tore it because your shoulder was out of alignment, which caused your pelvis to rotate, which rotated your knee out of alignment, putting too much stress on the medial aspect of your knee, especially your medial meniscus. When you lunged for the ball, you increased the strain on the inside of your knee, which was already under strain because of the existing postural rotation. The action that tore the meniscus was merely the last straw. That's your why. Your torn meniscus was an accident waiting for just the right (or wrong) amount of stress, which you discovered while playing tennis.

No doctor or physical therapist that I know or have ever come across will tell you your shoulder was the ultimate cause, and there's definitely no doctor in the world who will give you exercises to solve your shoulder misalignment to help your knee. That's okay; it's neither expected nor what they've been trained to do. But if you don't restore proper alignment to your shoulder, even after knee surgery (if it comes to that) and the ensuing rehab, you've only temporarily solved the symptom, not the problem. Your postural stress is still compromising that repaired knee and every other joint above and below it. It might also be impeding your body's ability to heal.

When the stimulus that caused the pain isn't removed, energy, blood flow, and range of motion might not have been restored. All three can hinder proper healing.

# Chapter 6

## INTERCONNECTED

By now, you should better understand how postural stress can lead to pain throughout the musculoskeletal system. But what about the other systems of the body? After all, if muscle or joint pain isn't your chronic issue, why should you care if you're misaligned?

You should care because postural stress doesn't just affect your muscles, bones, and joints; it affects your entire body. Let's begin with how it affects your respiratory system, particularly your diaphragm.

The diaphragm is a thin, dome-shaped muscle that forms the boundary between your heart, lungs, and other internal organs, like your intestines. It aids in inspiration and expiration and supports your spine due to the internal pressure it creates as it expands and contracts. The diaphragm is essential to your ability to breathe correctly, making it a vital aid in oxygenating every cell in your entire body, including your brain cells.

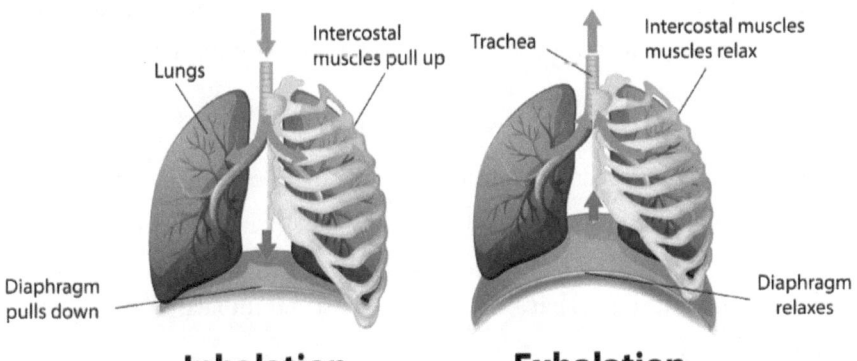

*The diaphragm during breathing*

Numerous postural imbalances can compromise the diaphragm's ability to function optimally. One of those imbalances is forward, rounded shoulders, which impedes the ability of the lungs to expand fully and the diaphragm's ability to work correctly. You can quickly test this by sitting upright and taking in a deep breath. Notice the depth and duration of your breath. Then, let yourself slump, allowing your upper back to round like the Hunchback of Notre Dame, and take another deep breath. Can't breathe as deeply? Of course not. Your rib cage can no longer expand, your diaphragm can't reach its end range of contraction or relaxation, and neither can your chest cavity or your lungs because they don't have the space.

In a real-world scenario, to make up for the lack of oxygen, people with rounded-forward shoulders or kyphosis (rounding of the upper back) are often forced to increase their respiratory and heart rates, putting more strain on the muscles and arteries of the heart and lungs. It also takes more energy to breathe faster and pump more blood throughout the body. Over time, energy expended in this way must be taken from somewhere else, like the immune or digestive systems.

Once your heart rate increases, your brain now believes you're under duress, and that kicks in your sympathetic nervous system, which is your brain's fight-or-flight mode. In this mode, your brain releases a cascade of stress hormones like adrenaline and cortisol, which further impede your immune and digestive systems, make you more irritable, and diminish your ability to tap into creativity, peace, and calm.

So, just by changing the position of your back, you've changed the function of your entire cardiovascular system, negatively impacted every muscle, organ, and cell in your whole body, potentially compromised your immune and digestive systems, and impacted your emotional state. That's a lot for one postural imbalance. Imagine having many.

No system is immune to postural stress. When muscles lock down due to misalignment, they can cut off blood flow, which impacts blood circulation. When the pelvis changes its tilt from neutral to tucked under or tipped forward, it affects the tension on the abdominals and intestines, which can impede the ability to eliminate waste. If the head moves forward of the shoulders (forward head posture), your head and neck muscles can tighten up and constrict blood flow and oxygen to your eyes and brain. A misalignment of the spine can impinge on a nerve, affecting the neurological system.

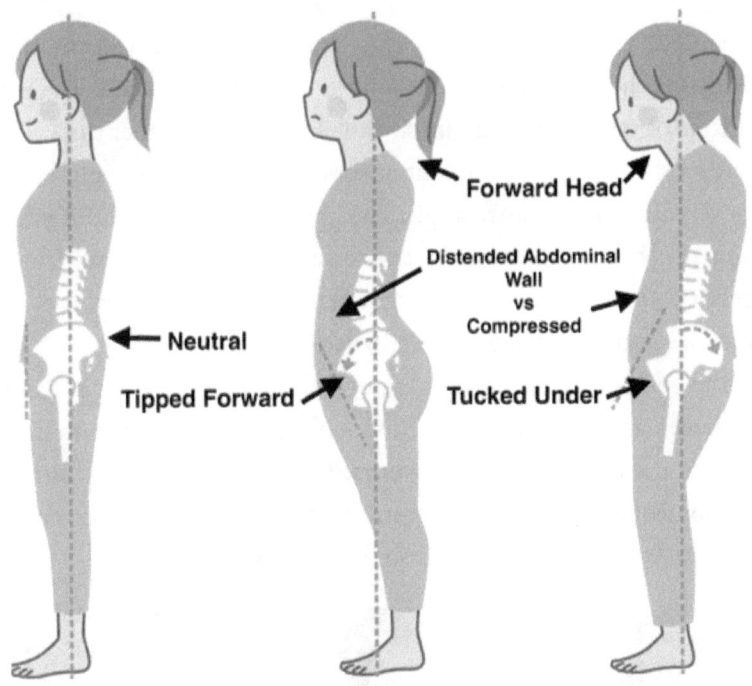

*Different pelvic positions affect everything from breathing to digestion and more.*

The message is that everything is interconnected, and if you think you don't have a posture problem, I encourage you to find out for yourself.

## Chapter 7

## A LOOK IN THE MIRROR

TAKE OFF YOUR shoes and socks. Your feet need to feel the floor directly for themselves without the interference of the shoe. The pros and cons of shoes will be an important subject for another time.

Also, throw on a bathing suit or shorts that land above your knees, remove your shirt if you're a guy, and throw on a sports top if you're a woman. If you're alone and want to see it all, go for it, but it's not necessary. (I once had a client threaten to completely disrobe so I could "see it all," to which I politely declined).

The goal is to see as much of your head, shoulders, elbows, hands, hips, knees, and feet as possible. Now, look at yourself straight on in the mirror. You should be able to see yourself from head to toe. You can also enlist someone to take pictures from the front, back, and sides. Again, make sure you can see yourself from head to toe in the image.

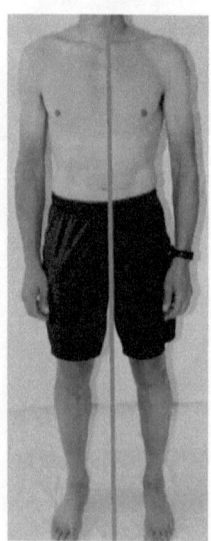 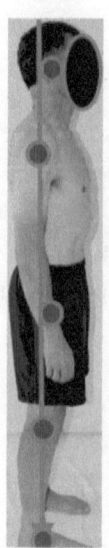 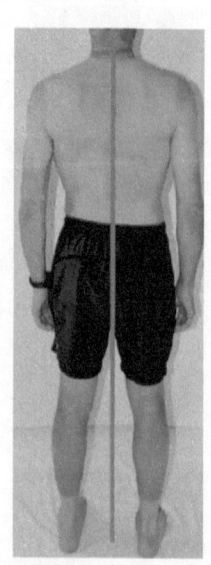

Whether looking at yourself in the mirror or at your pictures, begin the postural assessment starting with your head. I've included what each misalignment indicates in terms of postural stress.

- Does your head look straight, or is it off to one side?
    - » This indicates stress on one side of your cervical spine (the vertebrae of your neck) and a kinked neck, along with tension on one side of your jaw and in one shoulder blade.
- Do your shoulders look level? Is one shoulder higher or lower than the other?
    - » If your shoulders aren't level, imbalanced tension on each side of your spine could lead to stress on the cervical and lumbar vertebrae, resulting in neck pain, lower back pain, or disc herniations in either area.
- Does one shoulder appear to be rounding forward toward the mirror?
    - » With this imbalance, we're venturing into more muscular tension in one arm, wrist, and shoulder than the other. There's also stress in the upper trapezius, which is the area where the shoulders meet the neck. This is a common area of tension and pain for many people.
- Is your upper body straight, or does it lean to one side?
    - » We call this an upper-body offset. It means there's a lot of tension on one side of your back and along one side of your rib cage and waist. It's another common cause of lower back pain and disc herniations.

*Trunk lean called an offset.*

- Do your hands sit evenly at your sides, or is one lower?
  - » This is another indication of one shoulder dropping lower than the other. It means there's excess stress on one side of the spine, which could lead to back, shoulder, neck, and sciatic pain.

- Do you see the backs of your hands or just the thumb and the forefinger?
  - » Your hand position indicates the position of your arm bone. Seeing the backs of your hands rather than just your thumb and forefinger indicates internal rotation of your arm bone, which points to stress in your shoulders, upper back, elbow, and wrist.

- Does one hand look different than the other?
  - » You're simply identifying a difference between your

right and left sides, indicating stress in one shoulder or on one side of your spine.

- Does one hip appear to sit higher than the other?
    » If you put your hands on top of your hip bones, you'll be able to see this better. When one side of your pelvis sits higher than the other (see the front and back views in the previous pictures), it changes the position and function of the hip joint while putting stress on one side of the spine. This is another postural condition directly related to disc herniations in the lower back and especially to sciatic pain.

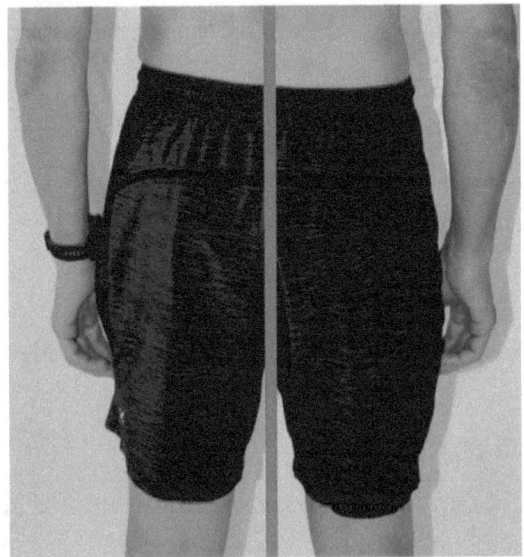

*Elevated and rotated left hip*

- Does one hip seem to be forward of the other?
    » Rotation in the pelvis stresses the lower back, the hip muscles, the knee, and even the foot.
- Do your kneecaps point straight ahead?
    » The kneecaps usually follow the position of the large

leg bone (the femur). Knees that point straight ahead indicate the femur is in a neutral position. If the knees point inward or outward, it means there's stress on each side of the knee, the hip joint, its surrounding muscles, and the feet.

- Do they look different than one another?
  - » Often, the knees don't point in the same direction, highlighting a right-to-left imbalance in the hip muscles and the muscles on each side of the spine.
- Does one foot sit in front of the other?
  - » This indicates pelvic rotation, where one side of the pelvis has rotated forward, causing stress on the spine and the knee.
- Is one foot turned out more than the other?
  - » Again, when this is present, the sides of the body are operating differently from right to left. There's also a difference in pressure and stress in each foot and knee.

That concludes the assessment from the front. Now, assess the side views.

- Is your ear forward of your shoulder?
  - » This is a telltale sign of neck pain since the head and neck muscles have to work overtime to support the head. Stress also occurs in the jaw, upper shoulder, and upper back muscles.
- Does your head look forward in general?
  - » This posture is related to stress on the neck and shoulders, headaches and migraines, jaw clenching, upper back tension, and lower back pain.
- Are one or both of your shoulders rounded forward?

- » Often very evident from the side view, rounding the shoulders creates an abundance of stress on the shoulder joints, the upper back, the neck, and even the lower back.
- Does the middle of your hip joint line up under your shoulder or over the middle of your ankle?
  - » If the hip joint is forward of the ankle and the shoulder joint, there's too much stress on the lower back.

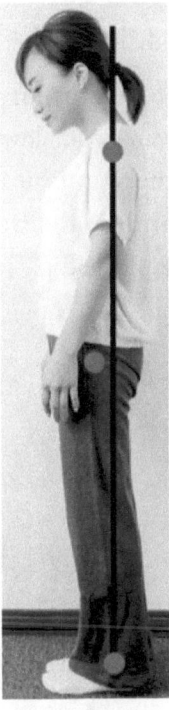

*See the hip joint (dot) sitting forward of the ankle and the shoulder.*

- Is your knee straight or slightly bent?
  - » If the knee is slightly bent, the hip joint's range of motion is potentially limited, and the knee may not glide properly when walking and running.

- Do you have a curve in your lower back, or does it look more flat?
  » Your lower back should have a nice curve to help absorb shock during walking, running, jumping, twisting, and turning. A lack of a spinal curve indicates a disruption in shock absorption and stress on the lower back. A flat lower back is a common reason for back pain, degenerative disc disease, sciatic pain, and even stenosis (narrowing of the spinal canal).
- Does your upper body look like it's leaning forward?
  » If your upper body leans forward of your hip joint, you're over-stressing your lower back, neck, and the front of your knees and hips. We call this forward trunk flexion, because the trunk is pitched forward toward the front of the hip.

*Forward flexion of the trunk. Notice the ankle, knee, and hip are on the gravity line.*

Finally, check out the back view. You may notice things in this view you didn't notice from the front view, like one hip sitting higher, one hand lower, one hand more in front of your body, and other minor differences.

Repeat the steps for the front view, but add one thing:

- Do either one of your ankles collapse in, roll out, or do they look neutral?
  - » Ankles that collapse are known commonly as flat feet and correspond to stress on the plantar fascia, the Achilles tendon, the big toe, and the inside of the knee. Feet that roll out are called "supinated" or "high arches" and create tension in the plantar fascia, the Achilles, and the outside of the ankle. Ankle sprains are common or more likely with this postural position.

Remember, the whole point of finding where your body is off is to gain a better understanding of why you have pain where you have it. It isn't bad luck or because you fell off a horse when you were five. You healed long ago. The pain indicates the exact location where your body is under too much stress due to the misaligned position of your shoulders, hips, knees, ankles, spine, or all of the above. By discovering these and then solving them, you can solve the pain.

Now, it's time to *feel* your imbalances. Close your eyes, take a deep breath, and connect with your feet.

- Where do you feel the pressure on your feet? In the middle, toward your toes, or your heels?
  - » This test measures where your hips and upper body are sitting in relation to your ankles. If you feel the weight more toward your toes, it usually means the

muscles on the back of your body are under stress. That includes the calf muscles, hamstrings, lower back, and neck. Your feet are also under too much tension, especially the arches and Achilles tendons. If you feel it on your heels, that indicates your hips have shifted forward of your shoulders and ankles, and you've rooted yourself in your heels to maintain balance. Low back, shoulder, and neck symptoms are common with this posture.

- Do you feel more weight or pressure on one foot than the other?
    - » This speaks to the weight distribution between your right and left hips. Ninety percent of the time, the side you stand on more is the side that aches first. For example, if you lift five pounds with one arm and ten pounds with the other, over time, the arm lifting more weight will be the first to conk out.
- Do you feel the pressure more toward the outside or inside of the foot or more in the middle?
    - » This question illustrates hip rotation. If you feel more weight on the inside or outside of one foot than the other, it means one hip (usually the side of the foot that collapses in) has rotated forward. One-sided pain usually results from this imbalance. It's called a rotational imbalance. Nerve pain down one leg, meniscus tears or knee pain, bunions, back pain on one side, imbalances in the range of motion between your shoulders, and a difference in range of motion or pain when turning your head side to side are all signs of rotational imbalance.
- Take a deep breath. Does it all come from your upper

chest, or did your stomach move out and expand as you inhaled?

- » You might have noticed when you inhaled that it mainly came from your upper chest rather than a combination of your chest and lower abdomen. If that's you, it indicates possible chronic tension in your upper shoulders and lower back and that your upper back is a little tight. It also indicates you're holding onto some emotional stress in the form of worry, fear, or anxiety.

- Squeeze the muscles on the front of your upper thighs (the quad muscles) five times, relaxing between each squeeze. As you squeeze them both, do they squeeze equally?

- Squeeze your butt muscles five times. Do they squeeze equally? Can you squeeze them at all?

  - » The previous two questions test the extensors of the knee and hip joints. The thigh muscles straighten the knee, while the glute and hamstring muscles bring the thigh bone behind the body when walking. The two sets of muscles represent a balance between the front and back sides of the body. A right-to-left imbalance indicates pelvic misalignment, which is consistent with one-sided back or hip pain, among other ailments on one side of the body.

- Squeeze your shoulder blades together several times, relaxing in between each squeeze. Can you squeeze them together easily, and do they feel equal?

  - » If you're having trouble squeezing your shoulder blades together, your upper back is out of position and holding way too much tension. Upper, mid, or lower back pain is usually the result, along with tight hamstrings and a stiff neck. Shoulder, wrist, and elbow ailments are also common, because the mobility of your shoulder blades is crucial for full shoulder motion.

When you squeeze the shoulder blades, inequality indicates that one shoulder has moved out of position more than the other, and your spine and pelvis have rotated out of their neutral alignment. Again, one-sided aches and pains are possible just about anywhere when this imbalance is present.

The potential symptoms listed aren't the only ones possible by any means, but they're commonly associated. I'm not saying you'll experience any of them; I'm only pointing out some of the points of postural stress when these imbalances are present. Everyone has postural stress, but not everyone has pain. As I've listed before, there are a variety of other factors that add to postural stress, including, and especially, past or present emotional turmoil.

Most people have a combination of imbalances. For example, uneven retraction of the shoulder blades goes with uneven contraction of the thigh and butt muscles. They all correlate with a lack of equal weight-bearing in your ankles, knees, and hips. Forward head posture almost always corresponds to hips that have swayed forward, and shoulders that have rounded forward with them.

Please don't fret; I'll say again that everyone has imbalances, and most of us have a combination of multiple imbalances. These tests aren't designed to make you feel defective; they're simply a starting point and a way to connect with your body.

Hopefully, they also shed some light on why you're experiencing pain. Most people I work with never knew their left and right sides were operating differently, not to mention *that* differently.

Doctors and most other therapists don't teach you these things because most aren't taught to consider them. They're focused on the symptom in front of them—the major fire—rather than all the little fires feeding it. I'm intentionally using the word "symptom" here because that's precisely what back pain, disc herniations, neck pain, arthritis, torn muscles, and torn menisci are. They're symptoms of misalignment at the very least and products of emotional stress piled on top of that misalignment more often than not.

Whatever you discovered during the tests, you're now armed to take more responsibility for your health than you were before. These imbalances are fixable, but most people believe it's the doctor's or health practitioner's job to fix them.

Now that you know more about postural stress and where your body is stressed in particular, you know more than anyone else about your body. You are the expert, and with the CARE exercises (Correcting, Aligning, Rebalancing, Exercises) to come, you can take the appropriate steps to begin the healing process.

Please don't misunderstand; doctors and health practitioners can put you back together, but they're creating the right conditions and space for your body to heal itself.

Even when you break a bone, the doctor resets it and lets the body's inner healing wisdom run its course. You heal yourself due to the innate power within that restores, renews, and revitalizes when the right internal and external conditions are met. The internal conditions are belief, expectation, freed-up emotion, determination, and energy. The external conditions are freeing your body from postural and emotional stress and, sometimes, help from the right people at the right time. The more information you have about your body, the more likely you are to make the right health decisions.

You can also work better with your doctors and health practitioners as partners and participants in solving your health challenges. Finally, the more you understand the cause of any pain you're experiencing, the less fear and uncertainty you'll have about it, allowing your body to heal unencumbered by doubt.

## Chapter 8

# ORIGINS OF IMBALANCE

Now that you've uncovered some of your imbalances, it's important to understand where they came from so that you don't continue to reinforce them or create new ones.

How do these imbalances get there in the first place? There are a variety of factors and possibilities, including if you:

- Went to school or work and had to sit most of the day
- Carried a backpack or bag on one shoulder every day
- Played sports
- Carried kids on one hip (mostly a mom thing)
- Developed a habit of sitting and standing more on one hip
- Consciously or subconsciously imitated the way a parent stood or walked
- Wrote, ate, brushed your teeth, and carried out other tasks with one dominant hand
- Played a one-sided instrument like the guitar, violin, flute, or the like
- Have unconscious habits that favor one side
- Work in an imbalanced profession (dentists, for example, who constantly bend and twist to one side)

Please don't interpret this list as exclusive or as something you've done wrong. Every item simply indicates that you're human, have lived a life, and are still here. The list is merely a nonjudgmental summary of some of the ways we become imbalanced and asymmetrical.

To understand each item listed, we don't need to tackle it individually. Instead, we can cover all imbalances with one basic concept: adaptation.

Simply stated, our bodies adapt to the stimulus we give them. If we repeatedly throw a ball, we develop the neural pathways and the muscle coordination to throw it better in a matter of days or weeks. In a similar manner, if we carry a backpack on one shoulder, play an instrument, hop on one leg, hone a golf swing, kick a soccer ball, ride a bike, or engage in an unconscious habit enough times, our nervous systems and our muscles adapt to it. Once adaptation has kicked in on any imbalanced motion or habit, the muscles change their tensions, our bodies change position, and the rest is history.

I once had a colleague who couldn't figure out why one of his clients was experiencing severe back pain. They were several weeks into treatment without any results, so he asked his client if he could visit him at work. This man sat at his desk on the phone most of the day, which didn't explain the pain in itself, but the way he answered the phone did. His phone was on the far side of his desk, so every time it rang, the man had to reach across his body and over his desk to answer it. As he reached, his body twisted to one side over and over again. My colleague grabbed the phone, moved it within short reach directly in front of his client, and a few days later, the pain disappeared, never to return. It was a clear lesson in adaptation and the imbalances we can create when we're not conscious of our repetitive movements.

Everyone has imbalances to some small or large extent. It's not a matter of if you have imbalances; it's how much they impact your body and your life. Despite the presence of some major misalignments, not everyone suffers from nagging injuries or chronic pain.

Our bodies are incredibly resilient and can handle a great deal of postural stress, which begs the question as to what creates the tipping point into pain. We'll examine the impacts of emotional stress soon, but pain and injury become a thousand times more likely, regardless of the joint's position, if the joint becomes limited in any way due to tightness.

A tight joint is a restricted joint, and a restricted joint is an injury waiting to happen. Therefore, mobility—the ability of the joint to move freely through its full range of motion—is crucial to its health. Let's examine four distinct conditions that can lead to restricted muscles and joints, which can then result in pain:

- Underuse
- Injury
- Repetitive habits
- Poor strength training

## Underuse

Dentists have a saying: "Only brush the teeth you want to keep." The same holds true for our bodies. We should only use the muscles, bones, and joints we want to keep. It's not that they'll disappear altogether; they'll just become weak, dysfunctional, and prone to injury if we neglect them, which happens often. Take many people's average day as an example:

They wake up and sit to read the news while sipping on a cup of coffee; sit in a car, bus, or train on the way to work; sit at the desk for three to four hours in the morning; sit somewhere for lunch; sit at work for three to four more hours in the afternoon; sit again on the ride home; sit on the bike at the gym for exercise; sit for dinner and then for several more hours watching television.

Here's the good news: Despite its poor publicity over the years, sitting isn't the problem. A lack of stimulus to wake up the muscles that oppose sitting is the problem. I believe you can sit all day as long as you do enough to stimulate the muscles that aren't being used—the glutes, the extensor muscles of the spine, the shoulder extensors, and shoulder rotators, to name a few.

Joints and muscles need to be reminded of their range of motion often, or they'll tighten up. If you've ever been in a cast or had to be immobilized for any length of time, then you know how long it can take to restore the full range of motion to a shoulder, hip, knee, or ankle. You want to take all your major joints through a full range of motion several times a week at minimum. Every day is ideal.

It doesn't take long for a joint to become restricted. For some joints, it can be days, for others, weeks. Most muscles begin to weaken from underuse in a matter of days. If you're laid up on your back for weeks, it might take just as long or longer to restore your previous strength.

If you have to sit for work all day, make sure you're getting up every thirty to sixty minutes to move. Walking is good, stretching is great, and the combination of the two is ideal.

Unfortunately, if you think you've got it covered because you're a swimmer, cyclist, or runner, you don't. Repetitive motion sports only train the muscles needed for the sport, not all the muscles. For example, running is fantastic for almost every system in your body, but the muscles responsible for rotation, side-to-side movement, bending forward, and reaching up aren't being used. The same is true for cycling. Your knees, hips, spine, and shoulders receive very little rotational stimulus, no side-to-side movement, and not a lick of end-range motion in any joint, especially the hips and the spine.

Swimming is a fantastic activity, too, but you might as well be walking on the moon. Your load-bearing joints, glutes, and hamstrings aren't being stressed because of your weightlessness and horizontal position in the water.

Please don't misunderstand. All these activities are fantastic for your health, but they aren't enough to keep your body fully functional, because they only use certain muscles and joints to accomplish the job, while the others sit on the sidelines. That doesn't mean you should avoid them; it just means you want to supplement your activities with movement that requires different muscles. In addition to your regular cardio workout, you might add a stretching routine, yoga class, dancing, or some other activity that uses your whole body. As long as you're doing something that takes your hips, shoulders, knees, ankles, and spine through their full ranges of motion a few times a week, you're likely doing enough to maintain muscle and joint mobility. My wife and I lead a weekly functional range of motion class I call, "Sunday Stretch" that we started during COVID for this very purpose. It's designed to stimulate all the muscles and joints through a full range of motion, balance, and strength. You don't need a special class, though, you just need to vary your activity and let your body be your guide.

## Injury

In the last section, I used the example of wearing a cast to show how a joint can become tight from lack of motion over weeks or months. Injury to any muscle or joint can restrict full motion with or without a cast and lead to long-term imbalances in the body. Imagine you tore one of your rotator cuff muscles in your shoulder as I did years ago. Your brain will do everything it can to protect your shoulder, including limiting the range of motion until the injury is healed. However, full motion isn't always available after it heals because of scar tissue or as a result of not moving for weeks or months. It took me a full year to restore full motion to my shoulder after the injury, and it wasn't easy. Restoring full motion is essential, though. If you don't, there are always consequences to other muscles and joints that have to compensate.

If I hadn't restored full motion to my shoulder, when I reached overhead to serve a tennis ball, my upper body would have had to bend to the side, or my back would have over-arched to compensate for my poor shoulder mechanics. Both compensations would have put my back at greater risk of injury.

*Notice the upper body has shifted left as the arm is about to reach overhead.*

It's also imperative to restore full motion to your knees and hips after injury or surgery. I can't tell you how many people I've treated for back pain who were hurting because one of their knees didn't straighten all the way or one hip stopped short of its end range of motion. How that works is for another book on joint mechanics, but the theme is compensation, just like bending to one side while reaching overhead when the shoulder is limited.

If you have chronic back, knee, or hip pain and have had an injury or surgery to either shoulder, ankle, knee, or hip in the past, you absolutely have to see a physical therapist or joint specialist to make sure you restore full extension to that joint. If not, I estimate that 90 percent of the time, those imbalances will lead to other pain sometime down the road if they aren't already wreaking havoc somewhere in your body.

Here is one exercise that will help you restore knee and hip joint extension and two that will restore full shoulder motion. Skip them if they increase pain or if you already know you have full motion in both joints.

## Lying Supine with Elevated Heel (for Knees and Hips): 10 Minutes

Lying on your back, legs straight, heels on the edge of a chair or couch, tie a belt or yoga strap around your feet so you can relax your feet out on the strap while keeping your feet pointing straight up. Do not hold your feet straight; let the strap hold them for you so you can relax your hips entirely. Relax your upper body and keep your arms out to your sides with your palms up. You should be totally relaxed. Hold for 10 minutes.

## Elevated Arm Stretch with Bent Elbows: 5 Minutes

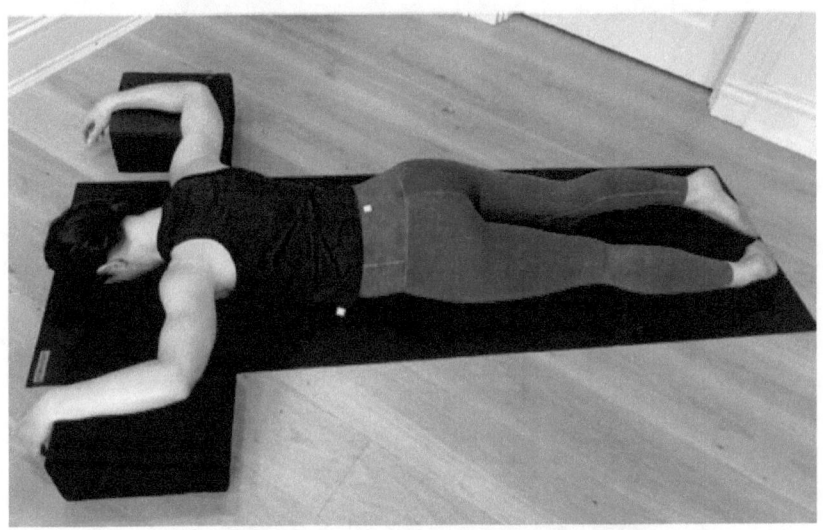

Lie on your stomach with your forehead straight down on the ground. Place your arms on two equally sized yoga blocks, pillows, or shoe boxes. Your elbows should be elevated anywhere from two to ten inches off the floor. You should feel a mild stretch across your chest or shoulder, so choose the height based on the stretch. There should be no pain. Pigeon-toe your feet and relax. Hold for 5 minutes.

# Elevated Arm Stretch with Straight Arms: 30 Seconds Each Position

Place your hands on two yoga blocks, equally sized pillows, a stack of books, or shoe boxes. Lock out your elbows, make a fist with your thumbs pointing up toward the ceiling, and rotate your thumbs out. Pigeon-toe your feet and relax your heels out. Keep your forehead straight down on the floor (don't turn your head). Hold each position for 30 seconds. Begin with the position that feels the most comfortable. Skip any position that causes pain. Your hands should be zero (no pillows) to six inches off the floor. Base the height on what feels comfortable for your shoulder.

## Repetitive Habits

Sitting is a repetitive habit for your hips, lower back, and hamstrings, because the muscles on the front of your body are chronically shortened. As I stated, that isn't necessarily a problem as long as you provide your body with the opposite stimulus to balance it out, but that's why it's important to move often. The muscles on the front of your body, such as your hip flexors, quads, and stomach muscles, all need to be lengthened, while your back muscles and glutes need to be shortened. Our bodies are all about balance.

As I mentioned in the section on underuse, sports can be repetitive habits, too, because they use the same muscles repeatedly. For example, running can lead to chronic tightness in the lower back, hips, and hamstrings. Cycling can lead to short and tight hip flexors, soccer can lead to tightness in the dominant planting leg, and weightlifting can lead to short and tight anything (more on that in a second).

It's important to be aware of how you stand, too. Most people stand on one leg most of the time. You can test this by standing up and shifting your weight onto one leg. Does that feel foreign, or is it comfortable? Now, shift your weight to the other leg. Which leg feels more normal to stand on?

Ninety-nine percent of the time, the leg you stand on more often becomes tighter in the hip, hamstring, thigh, or calf, which makes sense because you're using these muscles more.

We're designed to stand on both feet equally, but we learn to habitually favor one leg after injuries, from mimicking our parents, or after carrying kids on one hip for years.

We can also develop tightness in muscles or joints because of our professions. If you have to use the same hand for your job, twist to one side constantly, be in a cramped position, or engage in any repetitive movement for any length of time, tightness can set in. That doesn't necessarily mean you should quit your job; it just means you need to balance it out.

## Poor Strength Training

Poor strength training programs and bad technique during training are two of the leading causes of pain and injury in my clinic. I'm not referring to acute conditions; I mean the types of injuries and pain that build up from weeks, months, and years of reinforcing dysfunctional movement patterns and postural imbalances.

In my book *Ageless, Painless Tennis*, I told the story of one of my sixteen-year-old clients whose parents brought him in because he couldn't straighten his elbows. He had spent the summer doing bicep curls and bench presses with his friends without stretching or varying his routines enough. Within months, his arms looked like they were permanently stuck in a bicep curl position. His chest and arm muscles were so tight that it took about two months before he straightened out.

Every time I go to the gym, I see pelvic and scapular imbalances being reinforced, rounded shoulders becoming more rounded, and flexibility dwindling as the same muscles and joints are stimulated by the same weights and movements. Don't let that be you.

Vary your strength routines and exercises. Don't do bicep curls, bench presses, ab crunches, or any strength exercise for every workout or even more than two times a week. You can hit the gym every day if you really want to, but make sure you're doing different exercises every day.

Your nervous system needs varied motion and stimulus, and so does your brain, so mix up free weights with bodyweight exercises and machines. Try spinning one day, hiking the next, and working out with your trainer the next. Your brain and body will thank you, and you might save yourself a trip to the pain clinic.

## Chapter 9

# A Recipe for Pain

I HAD BEEN negotiating with another party to buy my exercise therapy clinic, and we had finally come to an agreement. I had one week to sign the contract. Out of nowhere, I woke up days before I was about to sign on the dotted line, and my neck, right at the base where it connects to my shoulders, felt like it had slipped out of place. I could barely turn my head, and if I tried to look up, it felt like my neck was going to break. I have never had this pain before or since.

Neck pain can often be related to feeling the burden of the weight of the world on your shoulders, but it can also revolve around fear. Specifically, for me, it was about the fear of having to decide on a definitive course of action. I was excited about selling my business and moving on, but I was terrified of leaving a company and a business I had built over the last fifteen years. I was feeling both the pull to stay and the push to leave, and I was completely unsure of what the future would hold. Everywhere I looked brought a sense of insecurity and the unknown, even though I consciously knew I was ready to move on. Luckily, I was able to mitigate the pain with some targeted exercises, but it didn't completely disappear until right after I signed the contract. Now I know why.

I can't tell you how many clients threw out their backs for the first or twentieth time, strained their necks, pulled a hamstring, herniated a vertebral disc, experienced digestive issues and migraines, or went into muscle spasms somewhere all because of a stressful life event.

They almost always blamed the activity they were doing, old

age, genetics, or bad luck, but the real reason is they were a postural accident waiting to happen.

They were misaligned with tremendous amounts of postural stress that hadn't broken through to physical pain until then. The imbalanced posture was akin to a crack in a dam ready to burst, and the emotional strain was the earthquake that broke it wide open.

As I mentioned earlier, I've come to believe most physical pain can be attributed to two things: postural and emotional stress, or PEST for short. We can add nutritional stress, like not getting enough or the right kinds of nutrients, and viral stress in the form of the flu, a cold, or some other illness, but these can be solved with the help of the right food or a good doctor. PEST, on the other hand, is up to us to solve ourselves.

Stress is loosely defined as any stimulus that causes physical, emotional, or psychological strain. In my twenty-plus years of helping people with acute and chronic aches and pains of all kinds, it's evident that any emotional and psychological stress accentuates postural stress.

This means that if any part of the body is out of position and, therefore, under strain, emotional stress will add to that strain to either produce or accentuate physical pain.

Simply put, we break at our weakest points. When you have postural stress anywhere on your body, that's usually the first place you'll feel pain when you're emotionally upset over something in your life.

Pain in the neck and top of the shoulders are common examples many people can relate to. How many people do you know who carry their stress in their shoulders? It means that they feel more pain in their upper shoulders and neck whenever they're stressed out.

Why would their shoulders be the target?

Every single person I've ever worked with who suffered from neck or shoulder pain carries their stress in their shoulders. For most, the reason is their head, neck, and shoulders are out of alignment. The head has moved forward in front of the shoulders, and the shoulders have rounded forward, indicating a major muscle imbalance that produces postural stress.

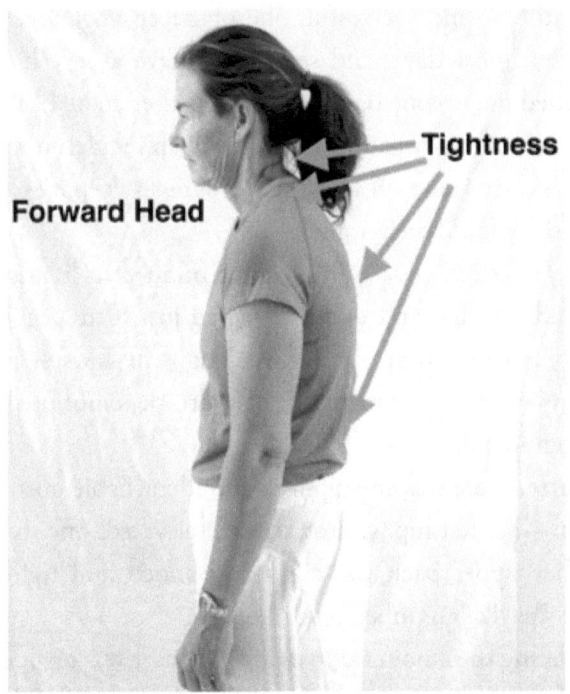

*Postural stress from rounded shoulders and a forward head creates tension in the neck, shoulders, upper, mid, and lower back. People can experience their emotional stress in all these areas.*

The symptoms don't usually stop there, though. Equally correlated are headaches and migraines, teeth grinding, jaw clenching, respiratory issues, and other symptoms of a misaligned head and neck coupled with unexpressed or unreleased emotions, mainly (but not limited to) anger and worry.

In the absence of an obvious postural imbalance, many others with neck pain are carrying the weight of the world on their shoulders. In other words, they feel responsible for everyone else's health, happiness, or well-being. Mothers are especially prone to this kind of emotional strain. Like Atlas, it's a big burden to carry, and neck or upper shoulder pain is a constant reminder of it.

I once worked with a forty-five-year-old woman who was

extremely athletic and successful. She practiced yoga several times a week, worked most days, and seemed to have a very happy home life. She called me up one day in agony over her acute back pain that showed up out of nowhere. She didn't recall an incident that set it off, just that it slowly came on and then progressively got worse by the hour until she could barely walk.

My first question was, "What's going on in your life right now?"

It turned out that an ex-coworker had just filed a major lawsuit against her and her company. Even though the lawsuit was utterly frivolous and eventually thrown out of court, the emotional stress had already taken its toll.

Of course, there was an apparent and identifiable postural reason for the pain—her left hip was rotated and elevated, one shoulder had dropped, her upper back was slightly rounded and tight, and her lower back was like an unbending steel rod.

Considering the amount of postural strain, it was obvious why her back hurt, but it hadn't been hurting before she learned of the lawsuit.

When I asked her to describe her feelings, there was a hornet's nest of unresolved emotions: fear over losing a lawsuit, worry over paying legal fees and what that could mean for her family, concern for her coworkers, and anxiety over potentially losing the company and a career she loved. As if that wasn't enough stress, there was the pain itself, which brought even more fear.

What if she couldn't get rid of the pain? What if it got worse? Was she broken? Would she need surgery? What if she couldn't exercise again? How would she care for her child and her family in this condition?

It's human nature to feel worried or anxious when the future becomes uncertain. None of us is immune to it. Like any fear, though, I've found the best solution is to rationalize it and face it head-on.

I began by reassuring her the pain was only temporary rather than a life sentence. Like her work emergency, it, too, would pass. Then, we discussed her concerns about losing her company and the strain it would put on her family and coworkers.

As she breathed deeply and gained some clarity, it became clear that no matter what, everyone would be just fine, including her. If she lost her company, she'd start a new one. If her coworkers lost their jobs, they'd find other jobs.

Her family had plenty of money to fall back on if needed while she built up another business, and her husband could easily manage their son while she recovered.

Whew! I could hear the sigh of relief as she let it all sink in.

Then, we addressed her postural imbalances. By the end of our session, she was already feeling much better. Within a few days, she was feeling 80 percent better, and within a week, she was pain-free. The real relief sunk in when she let go of control. She came to accept that the lawsuit and her ex-coworker's rage were both entirely out of her hands and that no matter what, everyone she loved, including her, was going to be okay. Once her fear dissipated, so did the pain. She has been pain-free ever since.

Have you ever been under emotional stress due to an event in your life and suddenly experienced pain somewhere? I can almost guarantee that where you felt the pain or where you're feeling pain now is where your body is under the most postural strain. Some sort of emotional stress was the catalyst to tease out the pain for the first or fiftieth time, even though the postural misalignment has been there all along.

Emotional distress hardly ever receives the blame, though. When any pain event occurs, most people blame their activity as the culprit. "I threw out my back while playing golf." "I was dragging my suitcase through the airport, and all of a sudden, boom!" "I bent over to pick up my child and suddenly dropped to the ground in pain."

These explanations are all too common and fail to recognize the real culprits. The injury was an accident waiting to happen because of the pelvic and spinal misalignment, but the detrimental emotional energy pushed it over the line. It became the literal straw that broke the camel's back.

# Chapter 10

## PUSHED OVER THE EDGE

THE LOWER BACK is one of the most common areas to experience PEST. In fact, 80 percent of us or more will experience back pain in our lifetimes (it's probably more like 99 percent), so I want to give a very specific explanation of how misalignment and emotions combine to produce lower back pain.

The pelvis is designed to be level and serves as the spine's base of support. When there's a muscle imbalance in the pelvic, hip, or spinal musculature, one side of the pelvis can elevate and rotate. The rotation or elevation creates twists and torsions on the spine, which changes how gravity is distributed through the discs and vertebrae of the spine.

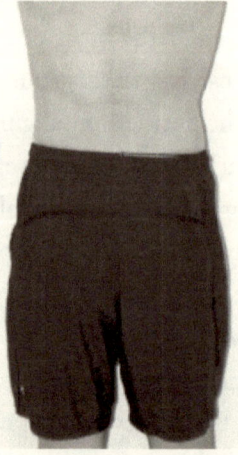

*An elevated hip creates a torque on the spine, plus imbalanced pressure on the spinal discs and vertebrae.*

Imbalanced pressure on one side of the spine can lead to a vertebral disc, the cushion between the vertebrae, to compress on one side while the other side bulges out. It's like squeezing one side of a balloon, forcing the opposite side to distend. Eventually, the walls of the disc can give way to the pressure, and the jelly-like insides can leak into the spinal canal and press up against the sciatic nerve. This is called a disc herniation.

If you've ever had any kind of back pain, you know how debilitating it can be and how devastating it is to your daily functioning, not to mention your enjoyment of life.

Yet, it's estimated that most people over the age of forty have multiple signs of wear and tear in their spines, including bulging discs, degenerative discs, and other conditions that produce no discernable pain. I want to highlight this critical point because just about every doctor, chiropractor, massage therapist, and health practitioner knows something you may not have considered: You can have a bulging disc, a disc herniation, stenosis (narrowing of the spinal canal), spondylolisthesis, degenerative disc disease, and almost any other condition of the spine, and not have pain. The presence of a clinically diagnostic abnormality doesn't automatically mean you will be symptomatic. This is true for almost every joint.

After extensive experience working with every back condition in the book, I can personally attest to this fact. If you've been diagnosed with one of the conditions above, then you already know this to be accurate; otherwise, how can you explain the fact that the pain comes and goes or that some days, weeks, or years are better than others despite the presence of the diagnosed condition?

Studies also back this up. According to a compilation of multiple studies gathered by researchers from the National Institute of Health, "Many cases of disc herniation are asymptomatic and found inadvertently on advanced imaging."[4]

---

[4] Dydyk AM, Ngnitewe Massa R, Mesfin FB. Disc Herniation. [Updated 2023 Jan 16]. In: StatPearls [Internet]. Treasure Island (FL): StatPearls Publishing; 2024 Jan. Available from: https://www.ncbi.nlm.nih.gov/books/NBK441822/

In layman's terms, it means that most people go about their active lives completely oblivious to the fact that they have a disc herniation until doctors discover it in an MRI.

This is one reason why the best doctors will not even attempt surgery for most spinal conditions until their patients have tried other interventions like physical therapy or alternative care. They also know there's nothing surgery can't make worse. Yet, even when a non-invasive treatment like yoga or acupuncture works to mitigate the pain, it usually doesn't solve the diagnostic condition. Stenosis, arthritis, herniations, and other conditions often remain. This is also true for necks, knees, hips, and shoulders. You can have a torn meniscus, rotator cuff, or labrum and not know it or even care because you're not in pain.

But if the presence of a potentially painful diagnostic condition in just about any joint doesn't guarantee pain, then what causes a pain flare-up? Often, there are a combination of factors, including:

1. Postural stress or misalignment over time (no, not age)
2. Emotional stress or repressed emotional energy
3. Excess physical demand on an imbalanced body
4. Brain protection response
5. A combination of any of the above

## Misalignment Over Time

We've already covered postural stress, but let me provide another example of how misalignment leads to pain. If you picked up a weight like you were going to do a bicep curl and stopped halfway, it wouldn't take long for your arm to begin to throb. It would quickly tire out and give you the message to drop the weight to relieve the strain. The culprit creating the throb wasn't the amount of weight or the bent arm; it was the weight on the bent arm over time, or, we could say, misalignment over time.

Similarly, a shoulder joint that rounds forward is out of position. If it remains out of alignment long enough, the muscles that protect and stabilize the joint will eventually fatigue in the same way. Aching, throbbing pain will likely follow to relay a message. In this case, the message is to restore the shoulder's neutral and ideal alignment.

By "time," I'm not referring to age. If your body shifts out of neutral alignment and stays there for days, months, or years, it will eventually let you know it's not happy, no matter how few or how many candles are on your cake.

## Emotional Stress

As I've argued, where pain hits you specifically often depends on where your body is misaligned and experiencing the most postural stress. Postural and emotional stress (PEST) creates an unholy synergy, causing pain and a predisposition to injury.

Emotional stress comes in many forms, including present emotional stress instigated by a current issue in your life or from unhealed past emotions you're still carrying around, including that of past trauma. Particularly stressful emotions—past or present—include:

- Anger
- Worry
- Fear
- Anxiety
- Depression
- Betrayal
- Resentment
- Bitterness
- Hurt
- Rejection
- Humiliation

- Rage
- Shame
- Shock

We have all experienced these emotions at some point in our lives. The more powerful the emotional experience, the more stress energy it can create, resulting in a more significant impact on our bodies with or without the presence of postural stress.

## Excess Physical Demand

If the wheels on your car are out of alignment, one of the tires will wear out faster than the others. If you're the only one driving and you don't drive that much, it might take years for that tire to wear out and burst. It might never burst.

If you start driving more often and then pile five more people in your car, that tire will wear out faster and pop sooner. That's excess physical demand.

If you take a misaligned back and expose it to weightlifting, carry a kid on your shoulder, go for a run, pick up a book off the floor, or swing a golf club, you're adding demand. We actually need appropriate "demand stress" to maintain every system in our bodies, including the musculoskeletal, digestive, cardiorespiratory, and immune systems. However, when we're emotionally compromised *and* misaligned, demand in the form of excess stress in any way—physical or emotional—can be the tipping point for pain to emerge.

I once worked with a thirty-year-old man named Tom who was complaining of shoulder pain. Every time Tom came to see me, I could predict what would happen before he arrived; he would still be in pain but would feel significantly better after doing the exercises. When I realized there was a distinct pattern during every visit and that I wasn't giving him bad therapy advice, I decided to dig a little deeper into his life.

On his fourth visit, I asked him if he was doing any strength training. I asked him on his first visit if he had been lifting weights, and he denied touching any weights for months.

By changing the word from weights to strength, I discovered several things. To be fair, he wasn't lifting weights as he had said, but he was doing one hundred pushups a day and as many pull-ups as his body could tolerate. When I asked why he was putting so much demand on a painful shoulder, he said he felt he needed to continue strength training to stay fit.

Tom demonstrated the full trifecta of doom—misalignment, excess demand on that misalignment in the form of pushups and pullups, and emotional stress in the form of fear. The fear was this: If I'm not in shape or don't look like Adonis (or Athena), I won't be attractive (and thus won't be loveable).

I assured Tom that three weeks of laying off the pushups wouldn't diminish his physical stature. It would, however, give his shoulder a much-needed break while he realigned his body and allowed the joint to heal. Thankfully, he heeded my advice, and when he came in for his fifth visit, he was finally out of pain.

If you're continuing to do something you know isn't good for you (like doing one hundred pushups on a painful shoulder), it's usually because there's a deeper motivation behind it. You're fulfilling an emotional need. Whether you're afraid to stop exercising because you'll be less attractive or are fearful that you'll gain weight, it helps to acknowledge that you're making a choice. Like Tom, you're choosing that need first and making it more important than eliminating the pain. We've all done it, but if you're doing anything that you instinctively know is delaying or impeding your body's ability to heal, I suggest you take a moment to rethink your choices. In other words, let your body heal first and then return to the activities you love.

## Brain Protection Response

Recent neuroscience breakthroughs show that chronic pain can often result from the brain misinterpreting safe messages from the body as dangerous. Even in the absence of physical damage to a muscle, tissue, or joint, the brain can still generate the sensations of pain. For example, John Sarno, who wrote the book *Healing Back Pain*, was one of the first to point out this mind-and-body phenomenon in people experiencing spine pain.

Essentially, the brain gets its wires crossed, but they can be uncrossed by changing some beliefs about the cause of the pain. Specifically, recent studies have shown that when patients accept there is no actual damage in the painful area, they can learn to let go of the fear and chronic tension they've been holding.

Out of fifty people employing this concept in one study using what's now called Pain Reprocessing Therapy, 99 percent reported less pain, and 66 percent reported they were pain-free by the end of the experiment.[5] Pain Reprocessing Therapy (PRT) is a system of psychological techniques to retrain the brain to interpret and respond accurately to body signals.

Cognitive Behavioral Therapy (CBT) and meditation are other techniques that can also help to rewire unhelpful belief systems and decrease stress to alleviate painful conditions.

You began to address your potentially crossed wires in the healing journal questions that asked you to examine your beliefs about your pain, and you'll continue to rewire your body and brain with the meditations and techniques later in the book.

## A Combination of Any of the Above

Misalignment, emotional stress or buried emotions, and excess physical demand are often harmless individually. Combined, they spell trouble. In some cases, big trouble. They're a ticking time bomb that *always* explodes sooner or later. Injuries, illness, disease, infections, hormonal imbalances, chronic or acute pain, or imbalanced and

---

[5] Ashar YK, Gordon A, Schubiner H, et al. Effect of Pain Reprocessing Therapy vs Placebo and Usual Care for Patients With Chronic Back Pain: A Randomized Clinical Trial. *JAMA Psychiatry.* 2022;79(1):13–23. doi:10.1001/jamapsychiatry.2021.2669

unfulfilling lives are the resulting refuse.

To avoid any of those unwanted effects, you should address the first two—misalignment and emotional stress—head-on and continue to clear up unhelpful beliefs about your body and your health.

Hopefully, you now understand that pain isn't always physical or emotionally based. It can be one or the other, or both. Other factors can also be at play, including too much demand on an imbalanced body and your brain getting caught in a negative feedback loop.

No matter what, it's imperative to uncover the emotional root of any pain because if it's impacting your body, it's affecting your life, thereby transcending the physical and touching on something unhealed or stuck inside us. Pain, then, can often provide an opportunity to discover those deeper emotional energies inside us that are keeping us from optimal physical, mental, or emotional health.

# Part III
*Your Inner Wisdom and Your Why*

# Chapter 11

## THE DEEPER MESSAGE

I PLAYED IN an adult basketball league for seven years. After over six years of playing without a single cut or bruise, and around the time my marriage was getting rocky, I suddenly got hurt every time I walked on the court. First, I jammed a few fingers, then a few more. Finally, I dislocated the ring finger on my left hand while reaching to steal a ball. The knuckle swelled to the point I couldn't wear my wedding ring. How's that for a symbol of marital and emotional stress?

The final straw came when I went for a loose ball and collided with my teammate, whose head slammed into my upper lip, almost knocking out my teeth and leaving a wound that required seven stitches. Instead of chalking all these injuries up to bad luck, I asked if the universe (or my subconscious) was trying to tell me something. As I meditated on the message, I realized that every time I was injured, I had come to the game emotionally distressed in some way over my relationship. Anger and rage were usually the primary emotions, and it wasn't just anger around the relationship being stuck, but anger at myself for not addressing it.

As a result, I came to four conclusions:

1. I needed to feel and process my anger.
2. I needed to acknowledge and respond to the feelings I was having about my relationship.
3. I wasn't having as much fun playing anymore and needed to move on.
4. I needed to respect my body and decide what was most important to my life (basketball or my fingers).

I was fortunate with all those injuries. I easily could have knocked out my teeth, and if I had dislocated any finger on my right hand instead of my left, I wouldn't have been able to play tennis for a very long time. As you can see, the knowledge I gained from the pain and various injuries was enough to change my life positively as long as I sought out the message and then acted on what I learned (which I did). If I had ignored my anger and the message and chalked up my injuries to "that's just how it goes in sports," I'm confident the universe would have gotten my attention in a way I couldn't ignore (like knocking out a few teeth, a torn ACL, ruptured Achilles, or something worse). I didn't want to wait for any of that to happen, and neither should you.

There are always warning signs that pain is coming. Most chronic pain begins with some kind of a functional limitation—feeling like you're not as flexible as you once were, a growing inability to do certain activities you used to love, or feeling like you need to limit your activity for fear of injury. The messages usually then escalate to a series of small niggles, aches, or strains—a random sore knee when jogging, waking up with a kink in the neck, or straining a back muscle or hamstring on the pickleball court. These minor inconveniences don't have to amount to anything, but they're all subtle messages that our hearts, minds, or bodies have been knocked out of balance. Unfortunately, we usually ignore our body's modes of communication or numb them with medication. It's understandable, given the busy lives we lead, the fact that most things heal themselves, and the general acceptance that pain comes with age. Yet, failing to heed the warning signs can lead to a message we can't ignore, like a major illness or injury that sidelines us for weeks or months or some kind of chronic health condition we didn't want or expect.

Like physical pain, there are also signs of impending emotional turmoil—overreacting to something insignificant, feeling overwhelmed, or suddenly needing to find comfort through food, sex, or alcohol. Predictably, we often cope with these emotional messages in ways similar to the physical ones: We bury, ignore, or deny our feelings and distract or medicate ourselves to dull them. Emotional pain carries no less a message than physical pain, though. The message is that if you don't address the source, you're risking your long-term health or happiness. The real takeaway, though, is that the physical and emotional warning signs usually appear at the same time. They're almost always interrelated. Therefore, you need to unveil the deeper message of the pain or, simply put, your why. This goes beyond your postural imbalances and emotional blockages and touches on what you need to heal inside you in order to heal on the outside. However, before you discover that, you must accept any pain as a gift the universe is trying to give you to learn more about yourself. It's an opportunity to heal yourself physically, but it's also a chance to learn how to create more connection, happiness, love, enjoyment, or fulfillment if you let it.

I can't tell you exactly what your pain or condition might be telling you, but for others I've worked with, it was a sign they needed to:

- Slow down and be more present
- Change jobs or careers to better fulfill what they're here to do in this life
- Find a better work-life balance
- Address what was missing in their personal lives, be it fun, passion, meaningful friendships, sex, pleasure, adventure, growth, or love
- Address their most prominent emotions like anger, grief, or loneliness
- Acknowledge how they had been abandoning themselves and their emotional, mental, or physical needs
- Heal past trauma
- Confront someone they're at odds with
- Let go of control

These are just some of the messages, or gifts, the pain provided so they could address and clear their emotional traffic jams. Understandably, it might be difficult to frame your pain as a gift, given the hardship and suffering your condition may have caused. Regardless, this is a crucial step to clear the resistance your reactionary, pain-adverse brain will surely mount against digging deeper into potentially uncomfortable feelings or life situations.

If you can't bring yourself to see this as a gift, pretend for a moment that it is. You can always return to resenting it later (although I hope you don't).

Looking at your pain as a gift will also enable you to leave behind any blame. We're masters of blaming others for our anger, hurt, pain, injuries, illnesses, and problems. Unfortunately, blame has never helped anyone heal from anything. The further away you are from it, the more you can find the answers you seek, and the faster you can begin the healing process.

Finally, you have an opportunity to open up the space to heal through a deeper understanding of what the physical injury or impairment might represent. Therefore, take your time to carefully consider the journal questions that follow, which can illuminate your path to optimal health in heart, mind, and body.

## Healing Journal

THESE ESSENTIAL QUESTIONS can help you uncover the message. Answer all of them if you can. If not, focus on the ones that resonate with you the most. You can always let the others marinate in your head for a day or two, and the answers might soon follow. Some questions might seem redundant, but even though they may sound similar, they're meant to approach your inner wisdom from slightly different angles in order to access your thoughts and feelings through a different perspective.

You have unknowingly been giving your energy and power away to your pain by ignoring the growth message behind it. Answer these questions to gain as much clarity as possible about why your health condition might be in your life so you can reclaim your power.

1. If your pain is a message, what could it be telling you?

Are you craving love and attention from a parent or romantic partner? Do you need to leave a bad situation at home or at work? Are there wounds from the past that need to be healed?

I've witnessed these exact scenarios in friends, clients, and family members who have struggled with pain. Maybe your pain is related to some sort of separation from love (the death of a parent, the end of a relationship, etc.). Write out whatever resonates with you, and then write out how you may resolve the situation to move on from the pain.

2. How or where in your life have you been abandoning yourself and your own needs?

If your body is speaking to you through pain as one of its many avenues of communication, then looking inward to see where you're not being true to yourself or even good to yourself is a great place to start. This is a moment when you consider that the pain on the outside—an aching back, gastrointestinal issues, migraines, etc.—might be a symbol of what you've been neglecting on the inside.

Maybe you're a busy mom and never have time for yourself, or a doting dad who gives everything to everyone except you. Or you've been neglecting your body by not exercising or overexerting it by exercising too much. Are you overeating or undereating? Are you trying to be responsible for everyone else's happiness? Perhaps you've buried yourself in work and let your personal life and your need for love and connection suffer. Maybe you dream about another life entirely and feel stuck in the monotonous grind of obligation, guilt, and longing. This is where you ask yourself, "What are my needs, and how do I begin to fulfill them?"

3. What's not working in your life right now?

Your life is a mirror of your thoughts, feelings, beliefs, choices, decisions, and more. When you really reflect on what's not working, like a relationship, job, or finances, you may hit at the heart of the emotional distress that's contributing to your physical distress. Another way to pose the question is to ask yourself, other than your health, what you are struggling with right now.

I described what my dislocated finger and other injuries from basketball were reflecting in my life and how they helped me address the discontent in my relationship. In a way, they were part of the impetus to seek more connection, love, and honesty with my partner and with myself. Acknowledging the struggle helps you to identify the stress.

4. In what ways has the pain been a gift?

There are pros and cons to everything, including chronic pain. Perhaps, through this experience, you're learning more about yourself and your body, you're learning to let go of control, you've been able to work from home, are spending more time with your kids, or are picking up a different hobby, among other benefits. Again, I'm not attempting to downplay your suffering or the negative things about your experience; I'm merely shifting your focus to help you realize there are usually upsides to pain or illness if you look at them honestly.

5. What are the unpleasant things the pain has allowed you to avoid?

You might discover more hidden upsides to your situation, which will help you further understand the message. For instance, maybe the pain is keeping you from being intimate with someone, which is bringing you a sense of relief or safety. Or maybe, because of your injury or illness, you can no longer clean the house, work in a job you despise, play a sport you're not really enjoying, or hang out with people who aren't positive influences in your life.

Perhaps the injury is allowing you to step away and reflect on your life so you can decide what truly makes you happy and what doesn't. That's a significant gift in itself.

Perhaps the pain is a message and an opportunity to begin living your life out of conscious choice and to free yourself from an unpleasant and unfulfilling obligation.

6. In what way could it be covertly benefitting you?

This one is tricky, but it's immensely important to understand what the injury or illness is potentially about. It sounds like the previous question, but it's actually very different.

Another way to ask the question is, "What's the hidden manipulation?" This is where you discover some of your not-so-pretty motivations, where the pain or illness is being used subconsciously as a manipulation to receive love.

I once had a client who was experiencing debilitating sciatic nerve pain that radiated down her leg and into her foot every time she stood up. As I dug deeper into her life, it turned out that as a result of her current disability, she needed to be cared for by her husband, who she had been feeling disconnected from for quite some time. The pain was serving as a means for her to get his attention. That was her manipulation and covert benefit. If left unacknowledged, she might have subconsciously wished to hang on to the pain as long as possible, which would have undoubtedly hampered her ability to heal and would have only been a temporary solution (and not a good one) to her loneliness.

This question will force you to examine if you're using the attention you're receiving through your condition as a way to feel significant or loved by friends, family, or a romantic partner. If you are, don't kick yourself for it. Instead, forgive yourself and recognize there are much more appropriate and empowering (and less painful) ways to connect to those you love.

7. How is your condition allowing you to play the martyr or victim?

For many people, their condition could provide the means to play the martyr or victim. Why would anyone want that? It could be a subconscious desire for attention or pity, which is another strategy for receiving what's perceived as connection or love.

Playing the victim could also be used as an excuse for a lack of success. This is common in sports where an injury can serve as a scapegoat. Instead of laying it all on the line, the injury allows for an excuse to lose. It's also common in the workplace, where a medical condition can serve as an excuse for poor work performance, a lack of success, or for avoiding work altogether.

Finally, if you're blaming someone for your condition, then you're automatically making yourself a victim. You want to let go of all blame so you can assume responsibility for your body and your life.

Total honesty and self-reflection are required for this question, but uncovering any hidden motivation is crucial to complete the whole picture. It might be the biggest key to determining the meaning behind the message.

8. What are you avoiding or not dealing with in your life right now?

This question speaks to a current fear, hurt, pain, or worry that needs to be resolved so you can find peace. Perhaps you're afraid of confronting your boss or dreading a difficult conversation with a loved one. Maybe you're at odds with a close friend, parent, child, or spouse and need to find a way to resolve the situation.

Whatever it is, you need to deal with it so that you can move on, and whatever you do, don't wait. As you now know, your emotions significantly impact your health. So, gather your courage, and take a leap of faith that speaking your truth will serve you in the long run.

9. What are you avoiding or not dealing with from your past?

The answer to this question is always relevant to the quality of your life, if not your current physical condition. If you haven't yet processed your anger or hurt from someone in your past, now might be the time to do so. There are techniques to do both in the section on the archetypes of emotion.

If you've suffered significant trauma or if you're not able to deal with the memories or emotions that come up, I encourage you to seek help from a professional or from someone you trust. I encourage you not to wait, though. You've carried this emotional baggage long enough and stuffed it down to the point that it's likely infecting your life in some way. I believe you're reading this now because something inside you knows you can handle it, and now is the time to start. Be brave and stay focused on the life and freedom you want on the other side, including the freedom that comes with good health.

10. What are you afraid of presently, and how is the fear draining your energy?

I told you about my experience with debilitating neck pain when I sold my exercise therapy clinic after fifteen years of business. The week before I was due to sign the legal document to assign new ownership, I suddenly experienced a massive ache and instability at the base of my neck. As I reflected on what I was afraid of, I acknowledged I was unsure about what my career moving forward would look like. I was also going to miss my work family and the purpose I woke up with every day, along with the shared overall mission that was bigger than me.

All in all, my major fears in this situation were:
- Was I doing the right thing?
- Was I going to regret my decision?
- What was I going to do next?

I'm sure you can relate to these fears if you've ever had to make a difficult decision about anything in your life, whether it relates to a relationship, money, or work.

I also had a fourth fear, which I think everyone can relate to: Was I going to be alone?

When you stop and reflect on what you're currently afraid of, you might discover you've been giving away a great deal of time, energy, and power to that fear, just as I did.

11. What are you punishing yourself for?

Chronic pain, injury, and illness can be subconsciously used as a form of self-punishment, so consider any guilt you may be feeling or if you're directing any anger toward yourself. Guilt—whether real or perceived, in our homes, schools, work, and society—is often followed by punishment, so why wouldn't we punish ourselves by creating a health challenge to pay our penance? We can also direct anger toward ourselves, especially when we're afraid to express our true feelings to someone else. Self-directed anger is an essential ingredient for many ailments, but we'd never know even to examine it unless someone pointed it out.

12. Are you ready to get well?

It doesn't matter what modality you use, how world-famous your doctor or health practitioner is, or how talented your healer is if you're not ready to be healed. You must be an active, responsible part of the solution, or there's a chance you'll experience limited results. This is not blaming the victim in any way, especially since you know by now you can't be a victim when accepting full responsibility for everything in your life, including your health—good or bad. However, suppose you're not done blaming your parents, doctors, yoga instructor, significant other, the guy who hit you with his bike, or using the pain for some secondary gain or manipulation. In that case, you'll probably put a damper on your recovery.

I worked with one client years ago in my exercise therapy clinic who came to me complaining of neck pain. She said she couldn't turn her head without pain. She also couldn't pay the full price for the session, so we worked out a price she felt she could afford, which ended up being about 80 percent off. Her husband had referred her, and he convinced her to come in after sharing his positive experience.

During the appointment, I gave her an exercise where I stood beside her, and she looked straight ahead. The exercise was stretching the front of her thigh. I asked her where she felt the stretch, and with that, she turned her head ninety degrees and declared she didn't feel it anywhere. I immediately registered the head turn (which she supposedly couldn't do) and changed the subject. At the end of the session, she said she might, maybe, possibly feel better, but it was hard to tell, and she booked for the following week.

Her appointment was right before lunch, so after she left, I also headed out to grab a bite. About forty-five minutes later, I ran into her outside a Banana Republic store. She was carrying about four or five different bags of new clothes from Banana Republic, Anne Taylor, and other stores. At least that explained why she needed a discount.

I smiled, said hello, made some small talk, and returned to

my office. I never saw her again.

She didn't call to reschedule or cancel her next appointment and didn't return my emails or calls when I checked in on her. Ultimately, I let her go and accepted that she had no intention of getting well. She had clearly been using the pain, or the excuse of pain, for some unknown secondary gain and wasn't ready to move on.

In any case, the story highlights the importance of being ready to heal on all levels of consciousness.

It's also okay if you're not! Love yourself. Then, gain some leverage on why you should heal this right now by acknowledging what it has already cost you, what it's currently costing, and what it will cost in the future if you don't change.

Sometimes, that's all the fuel you need to become single-mindedly focused on changing anything in your life.

13. Do you believe you can get well?

If you're hurting and there's some part of you that doesn't believe it's possible to heal, then you're telling yourself you're doomed. Of course, it isn't true, but your mind and body are playing it out as if it is. We tend to believe that once we have a diagnosed condition, there's nothing we can do. Arthritis, diabetes, degenerative disc disease, multiple sclerosis, fibromyalgia, chronic fatigue syndrome, and a host of other clinical diagnoses don't mean the end is near; they describe your current condition and symptoms. They can also be messages to change something in your life, whether that is to exercise more, eat better, align your body, heal past emotional trauma, ditch a destructive relationship, or something else.

No matter how dire your situation may be, I believe it's possible to heal most things with the right help, healing modality, and mindset. I've seen people crawl into my clinic with a massive disc herniation and walk out, heard of people around the world spontaneously healing from seemingly fatal diseases and diagnoses, among other miracles neither they nor the medical establishment can fully explain. I'm not trying to give you false hope here; I'm merely encouraging you to keep an open mind that anything is possible.

If any part of you doesn't think you can heal, dig into this limiting belief, discover where it's coming from, and throw it in the garbage where it belongs.

Too many people I've worked with have been told by one of their healthcare providers there was nothing they could do for their pain. They were "just going to have to live with it." It comes with getting older, or they could "manage it" with painkillers and physical therapy. The problem is that we put a tremendous amount of trust and, therefore, belief in these people who proclaim we'll never be whole again, and too often, it unnecessarily becomes true. One of my greatest joys in life is helping someone become pain-free who was told they were hopeless by someone who should know better.

By the way, if someone tells you to manage the pain, go ahead and manage it until you find another health practitioner who can help you solve it. I know there's a time and a place for it, but consider that there are so many different modalities, health practitioners, and therapies in the world. If one person can't help you solve your issue, it doesn't mean nobody can, so keep looking.

Now that you've answered these questions, hopefully, you've dug up some of the underlying roots fueling your physical condition.

Next, I want to explore emotions and their effects on the body more deeply and scientifically, starting with how they affect us biochemically. I believe it's essential to make the mind, body, and emotional connection clear so that you don't chalk this emotional stuff up to pseudoscience or new-age woo-woo.

## Chapter 12

# EMOTIONAL BEINGS

WHAT ARE EMOTIONS, exactly? On one hand, they're the wonderful, magical conduits through which we experience and interpret our lives. They make our lives feel real, root us in the present time, motivate us, and form the substance through which we connect to ourselves and others. We are luminous beings, and our emotions brighten or dim our light.

They also impact us physically. When we're sad, our bodies produce tears; when we're angry, our blood pressure increases; when we're excited, we're flooded with energy; and when we're amused, we laugh. We can't keep our emotions from being expressed physically any more than we can wipe the smile off a happy child's face. Yet, laughing and smiling don't explain the relationship between our emotions and physical pain, so we need a basic review of the nervous system to make the connection.

The nervous system can be divided into two components: the Central Nervous System (CNS) and the Peripheral Nervous System (PNS). The CNS is comprised of the brain and spinal cord, while the PNS includes all the nerves that have branched from the spinal cord to the rest of the body.

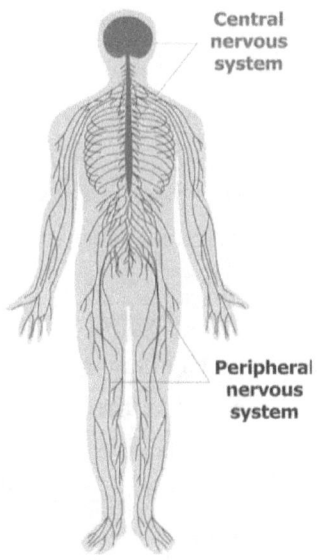

*The CNS (brain and spinal cord) and the PNS (nerves outside the CNS)*

The sciatic nerve is one example of a nerve that originates in the CNS and then exits from the vertebrae in the lower back to become part of the PNS.

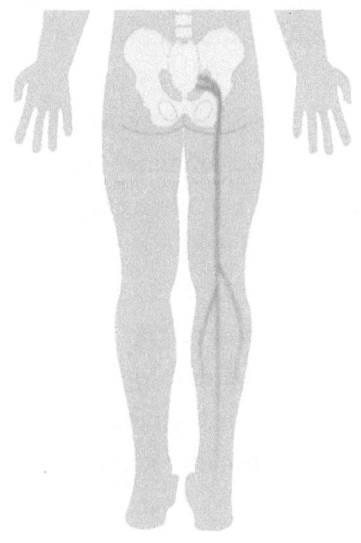

*Sciatic nerve*

There are thirty-one pairs of spinal nerves, each exiting on opposite sides of the spine to every muscle, joint, and limb. Every one of those nerves consists of billions of individual nerve cells called neurons, of which there are trillions in the human body. Some of these neurons secrete chemicals. These chemicals are called neurotransmitters, because they transmit neurological orders from the brain to various parts of the body.

Some neurotransmitters act as messengers to activate other cells, like muscle cells, and tell them to contract or relax. Other neurotransmitters signal organs like the heart to beat faster or slow down, and some trigger specific glands to release hormones.

Each neurotransmitter has its own chemical receptor, which are specialized cells that respond only to that particular transmitter. They work together like a lock and key. When the neurotransmitter key plugs into its receptor, it triggers the cell to perform specific jobs, such as healing damaged tissue, forming memories, activating muscles, and regulating blood sugar. Receptors are everywhere in the body, and together with their neurotransmitter keys, they communicate with literally every other cell and system to keep our bodies running smoothly.

They're the directors and modulators of our inner intelligence, effortlessly and efficiently running what we know as a living, breathing body.

If you've ever been prescribed any narcotic for pain relief, you were activating one of the most prominent receptors in the body—the opiate receptor. It allows the neurotransmitter endorphin (the body's natural painkiller and mood enhancer) to bond with other cells and work its blissful magic.

Drugs like oxycontin, morphine, and heroin all mimic our powerful endorphins and lock onto opiate receptors. They bind to receptors in the brain, spinal cord, and other organs to produce a state of euphoria and decrease pain. They come at a cost, though, because they trigger the brain's pleasure and pain center to want more, making them highly addictive.

Eventually, too much of a good thing can cause a surplus of endorphin-like chemicals in the body, which signals the body to restore balance by decreasing receptor sensitivity. To find the same high as before, we must then increase the amount of heroin or other opioids, making addiction or a deadly overdose much more likely.

However, not all neurotransmitters activate the brain's pleasure and pain center. Naturally occurring transmitters in the body regulate themselves and each other to maintain a delicate homeostasis, as each has an essential and distinct purpose to either enhance, excite, or inhibit a response from the cells they communicate with.

Scientists know of over forty neurotransmitters in the human body, each with a distinct purpose and receptor. Collectively, they influence or regulate every cell, system, and process in the body, along with their close cousins, hormones.

Unlike neurotransmitters secreted from nerve cells, most hormones are secreted by specific cells in organs and glands called endocrine glands.

You've undoubtedly heard of several hormones produced by endocrine glands like the testes and ovaries, including testosterone and estrogen, to name a few.

The endocrine system is interdependent and closely connects with neurotransmitters from the Central Nervous System. Together, they regulate growth, reproduction, motion, metabolism, heart rate, blood pressure, and everything else. Therefore, they make the mind and body functionally, biologically, and physiologically inseparable.

So, where do emotions enter the picture? Dr. Candace Pert, the neuroscientist who first discovered the opiate receptor and an early pioneer of the mind-and-body link, called these neurotransmitters, hormones, and their receptor cells the "molecules of emotion." That's because every emotion we experience turns into a neurotransmitter or a hormone that is carried to every cell in the body. That's how our emotions turn into the physical responses we experience every day, like laughing and smiling. Different emotions trigger different neurochemicals and, therefore, produce different physical reactions. Thus, the emotions we feel regularly can significantly determine the quality of our physical health based on their powerful chemical impact. That's why uplifting emotions energize us while constricting emotions like depression or sadness sap us of energy.

However, when it comes to chronic illness, disease, acute or nagging injuries, and pain, nothing compares to the effects of long-term exposure to the emotions of stress.

# Chapter 13

## WHY SO STRESSED?

Though we use the term "stress" often, it's important to know that stress can be defined as anything that pushes the body out of balance or homeostasis. Emotionally speaking, that means worry, anxiety, anger, grief, sadness, depression, loneliness, shock, fear, and undefined emotional pain, in which there are multiple constricting emotions under the surface we may not be consciously aware of due to past trauma or from emotions we've avoided and buried.

When occupied with these emotions consciously or subconsciously, our survival brain activates our sympathetic nervous system, otherwise known as our fight-or-flight mode. In this state, our brains believe there's a threat to our well-being and primes the body to run, hide, or fight. When in this survival and protection mode, blood is shunted away from the organs, muscles tense up to be ready for action, and cortisol and adrenaline are released. These two hormones act like the body's natural high-octane energy fuel. They prime every bodily system for immediate action, like a quadruple espresso, until the actual or perceived threat is extinguished.

But what if it isn't extinguished? Like a fire alarm that won't quit until the smoke clears, if the hurt, fear, devastation, shock, or other destructive emotional energy remains, the nervous system is hardwired to remain on constant alert. How might this happen?

- A stressful work environment
- Financial troubles
- Relationship stress

- Struggle with an important decision
- A stressful home environment
- The loss of a loved one
- Taxing personal obligations like caring for an elderly parent or a child with special needs
- Past trauma

These are just a few examples of common life stressors. Even our normal, daily lives can be stressful. Put yourself in the shoes of an average working adult: You wake up and immediately think about everything you need to accomplish for your day, frantically help the kids prepare for school, become stuck in heavy traffic that threatens to make you late for work, have to be on your game for eight to ten hours straight, hit another spat of traffic on the way home, jump on the exercise bike (which depletes energy reserves more), rush to put dinner together, put the kids to bed, and finally sit down to watch the news (which is always stressful). If you don't count sleeping (if it's even restful), most people spend about one to two waking hours out of sixteen blissfully tuned out to their stressful worlds via distraction through social media or some form of entertainment.

However, the daily stress of life is only half of it. Between regular responsibilities, there's also the constant ping of the phone with every text, emails that need responses, angry bosses, sick kids, difficult in-laws, struggling friends that need help, and a political and world landscape that isn't exactly reassuring. Add financial worries, relationship issues, or an aching body part to the mix, and there are stress hormones coursing through your arteries and veins like blood.

Incredibly, we adapt to our stressful lives and learn to live with a continuous deluge of it, but that doesn't mean our bodies like it. It's exhausting, and our bodies struggle to return to homeostasis, leaving cortisol and adrenaline circulating longer than normal. These chemicals are catabolic, which means they break down tissue over time to maintain a high enough blood sugar level so the body can continue to function on high alert. As they're broken down for energy, muscles, joints, and tendons then become more vulnerable to injury during sports or activities. In addition, digestion is impeded, the heart works harder, and the immune system is muted, giving foreign bacteria, mutated cells like cancer, and other germs a fighting chance to wreak havoc.

That's not nearly all. As tissue is broken down for energy, immune cells are sent to heal the damage, but since it's not functioning at 100 percent due to cortisol, they can't keep up, leaving the tissue inflamed. Unable to combat the growing inflammation, like an oil leak outpacing the cleanup crew, it can spread throughout our bodies. That can leave our guts, tendons, and joints chronically inflamed, leading to a host of potential symptoms like arthritis, muscle tears, tendon ruptures, nausea, heartburn, indigestion, diarrhea, constipation, lower abdominal pain, irritable bowel syndrome (IBS), dyspepsia (indigestion and upper abdominal discomfort), Crohn's Disease, Ulcerative Colitis, and more.

Healing requires energy, and stress creates a constant drain. Massive amounts of energy cannot be easily replaced, so eventually, the body hits a wall—no more energy.

You've experienced this type of fatigue temporarily if you've ever had a bad cold or the flu. When we're sick, our bodies use tremendous amounts of energy to fight the infection, which is one reason why we feel the need to rest or sleep (the state of sleeping also suppresses the release of stress hormones so the immune system can function better).

A whole list of common physical ailments could result from too little energy to keep the ship afloat, including chronic fatigue, insomnia, fibromyalgia, all sorts of digestive issues, muscle weakness, joint instability, migraines, hormonal imbalances, and aches and pains just about anywhere.

Remember that every emotion becomes a neurochemical capable of reaching every cell in the body. Therefore, no hair cell, skin cell, organ, muscle, or joint is immune to the effects of chronic stress, even the heart.

According to Dr. Daniel Brotman, professor and Director of the Division of Hospital Medicine at Johns Hopkins Hospital in Baltimore, "Intense grief, acute anger, and sudden fear can direct—sometimes fatal—effects on the human heart. And long-term emotional stress shortens lives by increasing the risk of heart disease." Dr. Brotman and his colleagues published a report called the "Cardiovascular Toll of Stress" in 2007[6], which reviewed multiple studies on the effects of stress on the heart. The evidence they discovered led to several startling conclusions, highlighted below.

- People who suffer from depression, hopelessness, or a pessimistic outlook are more likely than others to suffer from a heart attack and sudden heart death. They are more likely to develop conditions that increase heart risk, such as obesity, diabetes, high blood pressure, and impaired heart rate.

- People who suffer from chronic anxiety are more likely than others to suffer from a heart attack, atrial fibrillation, and sudden heart death. They also have a propensity for high blood pressure and an impaired heart rate, which further increases their heart risk.

- Emotional trauma such as the death of a spouse, mental or physical abuse, or PTSD increases the risk of heart attack and heart death.

- People with type D personalities (characterized by pessimistic emotions and inability to share emotions with others) and type A personalities (characterized by anxiety directed outward as aggressive, irritable, or hostile behaviors) are more likely than others to suffer from heart attacks.

---

[6] Sources: 1. Brotman, D.J. *The Lancet*, Sept. 22, 2007; vol 370: pp. 1089-1100. Daniel Brotman, MD, director of hospitalist program, Johns Hopkins Hospital, Baltimore.

- People with angry or hostile temperaments are more likely than others to suffer heart death.
- Acute fear, grief, startling, or anger can cause a "stunned heart." Wallops of emotion can also cause sudden death due to life-threatening abnormal heart rhythms.

Similar studies have been conducted on the effects of stress on the brain, immune system, intestines, muscles, and every other organ in the body that would fill an entire book. Suffice it to say that long-term stress is bad for us. Unfortunately, it doesn't have to be present stress. Stress from the past can also play out presently in our bodies. Before we dive into how that works, take a minute to assess the current stress in your body and your life with the following questions.

# Healing Journal

1. How often do you feel stressed?

2. What are the most stressful things (situations, obligations, people, etc.) in your life?

3. Where do you experience the emotions of stress in your body?

4. What can you change or eliminate to decrease the stress in your life?

## Chapter 14

# MEMORIES, EMOTIONS, AND AMYGDALAS

I'LL NEVER FORGET the day I broke my leg. I was nine and playing tackle football with some kids in my neighborhood. I distinctly remember where I was, who tackled me, the ambulance ride to the hospital, the doctors cutting off my jeans, and my mother and father right there by my side. The physical pain, intense fear, and those clear memories are permanently etched in my brain and can be immediately recalled decades later. It turns out there's a biological reason for this: Memory formation, pain sensations, and emotions all originate in the same parts of the brain.

The area is called the limbic system, which consists of several brain structures, including the amygdala, thalamus, hypothalamus, and hippocampus.

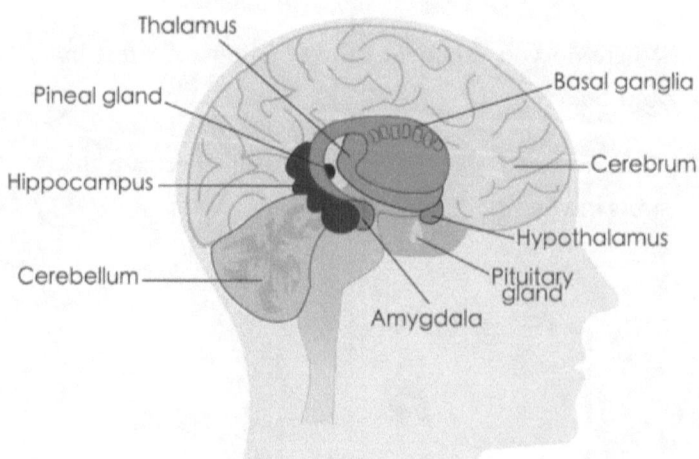

Think of the limbic system as the brain's emotional processing center. It is often referred to as our "emotional nervous system," because it's responsible for the production and regulation of our emotions as well as the learning and formation of new memories.

One part of the limbic system, the amygdala, is also responsible for the conscious sensation of pain. This means that the same part of the brain responsible for producing and regulating emotions and memories also interprets physical pain signals from the rest of the body and works to make them conscious.

Let me highlight how pain, memories, and emotions work with an example of stepping on a nail. When the nail punctures your skin, it activates the pain sensors located in the skin and muscles of your foot, which send electrical impulses to your amygdala. Your amygdala registers it like an event in a logbook, creates an associated memory to help you avoid nails in the future, couples it with an emotion like fear so you'll be afraid of stepping on nails, and then sends the electrical and chemical signal to the muscles and joints to move away from the nail. Then, you get angry and yell, "Stupid nail!" Of course, all of that happens pretty much at the speed of light. In this way, physical and emotional pain are immediately and intimately linked and logged into your permanent memory.

We accumulate oodles of painful physical memories throughout our lives—that time you were chopping parsley and chopped part of your finger instead, the day you sprained an ankle stepping off a curb, the debilitating stomachache and food poisoning you endured after eating contaminated food, and so on. These incidences of intense physical pain will live in our minds forever.

Of course, intense emotional moments also provoke lasting, strong memories.

Remember when your girlfriend or boyfriend dumped you for another, when you were bullied at school, or when you had an embarrassing moment in front of your friends? You bet your acetate you remember. Your brain won't let you forget, because those moments hurt like hell. So, you remember every sniffling, whimpering, screaming-in-your-pillow detail often decades later, all because some memories are placed in our permanent brain storage space to be recalled just in case we're ever in that situation again. That way, they can serve as red warning flags to guide you toward behavior that ensures your physical and emotional well-being.

Pain is pain to our brains, so it makes dang sure we remember it and steer clear of it in the future. It doesn't distinguish between emotional and physical pain or damage because it knows both can affect our chances of survival. To our survival brain, the powerful emotional pain of rejection, betrayal, loss, shock, and humiliation all pose a threat to our physical well-being. So, our brains engrain painful memories into our subconscious and conscious minds and then trigger painful and powerful emotions to remind us to avoid those pains in the future. The greater the pain, the more deeply ingrained the memory and the more powerful the emotion. The more powerful the emotion, the more powerful the neurochemical impact on the body. We can then say that our most memorable past physical and emotional experiences have not only shaped our fears, desires, beliefs, thoughts, and actions, but also our very biochemistry.

I bet if I asked you to recall five of your most painful emotional experiences, you could rattle them off in a heartbeat. I know I can. The question is, how did those painful experiences alter your biochemistry, and are they still altering it?

If you feel like your most painful memories are still haunting you and often experience the painful emotions that come with them, you're creating the same neurotransmitters and hormones (the same biochemistry) that you did back then. Your brain thinks you're still experiencing the event and, therefore, the emotional pain, keeping your body stuck in an endless state of fear, hurt, anger, disappointment, or whatever emotion comes up for you. Unfortunately, most people don't allow themselves to acknowledge or express those emotions, so they remain buried beneath the surface.

Eventually, that energy finds an outlet via a physical manifestation of pain or illness, making pain a very present reminder of trauma from the past.

# Healing Journal

1. What are three of your most intense memories from the past (good or bad)?

2. When you recall them, do you notice the present physical impact on your body? For instance, do you feel a physical rush of energy and excitement from a good memory or the opposite from a bad one?

## Chapter 15

# PAIN IN YOUR HEAD

"It's all in your head." Nobody wants to hear those five words, but it's often implied when the presiding healthcare model hits a wall. That's psychogenic, psychological, or psychosomatic pain. We've all experienced it in some form at some point in our lives, whether it was stomach pain, migraines, or even back pain that didn't have a clear physical cause.

Psychogenic pain—physical pain or illness caused by mental or emotional factors in the absence of observable physical injury—is widely acknowledged in the medical field. So is something doctors coined as "Pain Disorder," which is chronic pain experienced in one or more areas of the body due to psychological stress. It's one of the few times physicians accept the mind-body connection, though it's likely due to the fact they couldn't pinpoint a physical reason for the symptom presented.

I experienced my own significant, acute psychogenic moment one day in my mid-twenties after discovering my girlfriend had been unfaithful. I had broken up with her days earlier because I felt something in our connection was missing (I was about to find out why). When I walked up to her apartment to knock on the door, I saw them inside through the front window. Seconds after registering what was happening, my arms and legs suddenly went numb. I had to sit down outside for fear of passing out. It took me ten minutes to regain my focus and the feeling in my limbs.

What fascinates me to this day is that, at that moment, I wasn't that upset. After all, I had just broken up with her. My body clearly felt otherwise. I've never had that kind of physical reaction before, and thankfully, I never have since, and now I know what it's like to be in shock. I've also experienced first-hand how powerful an effect our emotions can have on our bodies, even if those emotions aren't obvious or are hiding under the surface.

After I broke up with her, I thought I had moved on, yet I was so shaken by the feeling of betrayal that it took me over a year even to consider dating again.

In the end, I learned three important lessons from this experience about emotions:

1. We don't have to be presently feeling emotional pain for it to register in our bodies.
2. Pain can last for years on end until it's addressed and healed.
3. Healing that pain is essential to living a life of physical and emotional freedom.

Unfortunately, once our brains have formed a neurological pathway linking a situation and emotion to physical pain—as I did when I reacted to seeing my ex with someone else—it's easier to reproduce that same sensation of pain later when in a similar situation, and it doesn't have to be that similar. For me, the mere thought of being in a relationship made my stomach churn for about a year. Unfortunately, we're no different than Pavlov's dogs, who were conditioned to salivate from the excitement of an upcoming meal simply from the sound of the dinner bell.

Our dinner bell is a person or situation that reminds us consciously or unconsciously of past hurt, betrayal, or some other painful emotional experience. Instead of salivating, though, we can experience other physical reactions, like a migraine, an illness, muscle or joint pain, or an acute emotional reaction, like fear, revulsion, or anger.

This is how emotional trauma from years past can spark current physical symptoms, even if you're not consciously reliving it. The memory of the trauma lives in your brain, encoded and ingrained by neurological pathways in your amygdala, reflexively reacting to protect you from current or future threats. Unfortunately, it doesn't matter if the threat is real. The subconscious fear encoded by the neurotransmitter in your brain is real, and it's readily released when encountering a situation that puts your physical or emotional well-being at risk.

Therefore, close relationships, loving connections, and shared intimacy can be challenging to obtain when our survival-based brains consider them a threat. That's where the metaphorical walls we erect around our hearts come from. And time doesn't always heal those wounds because emotions don't have a timestamp. They're chemically imprinted on the brain by the traumatizing event, ready to be recalled at a moment's notice.

Therefore, your current physical symptoms—muscle spasms, joint pain, injuries, osteoarthritis, chronic fatigue, and practically any other ache, pain, or illness I can name—can be the direct result of holding onto a past hurt, humiliation, blame, anger, resentment, envy, betrayal, abandonment, or trauma. Why? Because failing to heal from the past makes it present—neurologically, emotionally, and biochemically.

This is not new-age metaphysical banter. It's actual science. It's neurochemistry, biology, psychology, and physiology all rolled into one big, truth burrito that's hard to chew for some but easier to swallow if you accept that there's no such thing as a mind separate from a body; there are only the physical, mental, spiritual, and emotional energies that combine to make you *you*.

To emphasize this fact, let me tell you a story about a former client from long ago.

I once worked with a seventy-year-old man who was suffering from nerve pain, numbness, and tingling in both legs, often a sign of stenosis, which is a narrowing of the spinal canal where the nerves exit the spine and branch out to the limbs. He was losing strength every day, to the point that going up and down the stairs was becoming increasingly more painful and laborious. As I took him through various exercises to realign his spine and take the pressure off the painful nerves, I also asked him what the most significant stressors were in his life.

At that point, he had been retired for two years from a massively successful international law practice that had taken him around the world, where he was representing clients, winning most of his cases, and righting the injustices of corporate conglomerates. Over the last forty years, his job had given him daily purpose, meaning, self-esteem, and a profound sense of contribution.

You're probably thinking that as soon as he retired, he lost his purpose and meaning in life and tumbled into pain. All that is true. He was bored and felt like his life had less meaning, but his successful career, where he lost himself in his work, distracted him from his real pain.

His real pain was that he had been disconnected from his four children for the last twenty years after having gone through an ugly divorce. They had refused to see or speak to him ever since. From that day on, his job became a powerful distraction from his regret at how he handled the divorce, his anger at his ex, his feeling of powerlessness to rectify the situation with his kids, and his deep hurt that they may never want to see him again. His retirement unmasked the ugly truth underneath, with nothing left to hide the festering wounds.

That might have been okay if it motivated him to acknowledge and feel his loss, hurt, sadness, and regret. Instead, he kept it stuffed deep inside, and his outer pain—excruciating lower back, foot, and leg pain—became his body's only mode of releasing his inner pain that had been building up for decades.

I wish this story had a happy ending, but it doesn't. He went from one surgery to another and not only struggles with the same pain, but now his hips, shoulders, and knees are giving out.

He was never taught to feel his emotions. Most people aren't. He believed that admitting he had emotional pain was akin to admitting he was weak, which made him less of a man. He also vehemently refused to consider that his physical symptoms had anything to do with his past personal hurt, regret, and inner emotional distress.

Sadly, I understand. We're conditioned to think our bodies are our bodies, and our minds are our minds. If either one is hurting, we go to the medical doctor for one and the psychologist for the other. It's just one more cultural example of how we think about and treat the mind and body as separate entities.

## Healing Journal

1. Have you ever experienced, or are you currently experiencing, psychosomatic, psychogenic, or psychological pain?

2. If so, what do you think is or was the emotional root of your pain? Is it betrayal, shock, hurt, or something else, or is it hard to pinpoint and define?

3. If you can identify the emotion, write about your experience with it. Then, if you're able and willing, try to sit for several minutes and feel it—not to relive the past, but to purge the energy of the emotion. Feeling is healing. Try to feel it without being caught up in the past experience. Simply focus on the feeling and the emotion itself until it passes.

## Chapter 16

# PERSONAL TRAUMA

I'm a firm believer that if we're suffering from chronic pain or illness, we can't afford to bury our past painful emotional experiences when our bodies are screaming at us to acknowledge them. They're often the elephant in the room, stomping on our chests instead of standing in the corner.

The thing about trauma is that we all have it to some degree, because we have a past. Psychologists refer to varying degrees of trauma as "little trauma" or "little t" and "big trauma" or "big T." The two are separated to distinguish and honor the difference between being abused or majorly traumatized compared to the more common hurtful, frightening, or emotionally impactful experiences we all encounter throughout our lives.

Instances of little trauma might be having been bullied, humiliated, or harassed as a child or adolescent. They're all the deeply ingrained hurtful memories resulting from your interpretation of a parent missing your baseball games or dance recitals and even a parent ignoring or abandoning you.

Other relevant little t's came from memories of being dumped by a boyfriend, being embarrassed in front of your classmates, failing a major test that left you feeling like you were a failure, and so on.

We have hundreds, maybe thousands, of these moments throughout our lives, and they each affect us in some way. They may be microtraumas, but they're real and inside us, nonetheless.

I'm sure you can recount dozens of them if you set your mind to it, and there's a good chance the energy of the resulting emotions is still inside you. In that sense, we can define any trauma we're still holding onto as unhealed emotional pain, which most of us carry throughout our lives.

I remember being bullied by some sixth graders in my elementary school when I was just a fourth grader. One of them stole my backpack and threw it up on top of a tetherball pole. I retrieved it and decided that I wouldn't allow that to happen again, no matter what. So, the next time that kid and his friends tried to have another go at me, I tackled and wrestled him to the ground. I was sent home for fighting, but that kid and his bloody nose never bothered me again.

That decision to fight back stays with me, as does the anger at that kid. I hadn't realized I was still carrying it until I did an anger letter (you write down everything you are and have ever been angry at—see the chapter on anger) about ten years ago, and the memory popped up out of nowhere.

I dislike bullies to this day, especially the ones in the public eye, but as I cleared my anger, I also recognized that the kid had likely been bullied himself. When I brought it up years ago to a friend who also knew that kid, it turned out he had an older brother who was every bit as mean, if not meaner, than he was. I forgave him (in meditation), and when I think of the event now, the only thing that comes up is a memory without an emotional charge.

That experience is definitely a little t, but even that minor incident set off enough anger to influence my thoughts and feelings about bullies for decades.

Although most minor traumas don't affect us physically, they add to our unhealed emotions, making them relevant. As I mentioned, whether big or little, we all have some form of trauma in the sense that we have unhealed hurt, anger, betrayal, and shame lurking from our pasts and lingering in our present. You don't have to have been abused or in a war for it to be affecting you in some way.

It's important to buy into the idea that any unhealed emotional pain can manifest as a physical symptom. It doesn't have to, but it often does, and it *always* does if that emotional energy is powerful and left intact and unhealed long enough.

# Healing Journal

1. What little or big traumas from your past do you suspect are still influencing your life or your body now?

2. When you bring up those memories, do the painful emotions (hurt, anger, betrayal, fear, etc.) still surface with them?

3. When these emotions come up, where exactly do you feel them in your body?

4. If you can pinpoint where you feel them in your body, is this the same area where you feel pain or discomfort?

If you can pinpoint where you feel the emotion or emotions in your body, see if you can breathe through them. Notice them and feel them, but don't attach yourself to them. They're feelings and memories, that's all. You don't have to give them any more significance than that. Just breathe, feel, notice, and see if you can let their energy begin to dissipate and disappear. This can be a helpful technique to make the connection between your emotions and the pain you're experiencing while also purging the energy of a constricting emotion that's been negatively impacting your health and your life.

## Chapter 17

# ARCHETYPES OF EMOTION

Now that we've identified postural and emotional stress as two common ingredients that combine to incite chronic pain and you know how emotions play out physiologically, I want to give you some more concrete examples using real-life former clients to show how specific emotions can affect our bodies. I've changed the names and some of the details to protect their privacy, but the bodies, symptoms, emotions, and treatments are real.

Even if your symptoms differ, you may have many of the same or similar emotions that are impacting you in some way, so I encourage you to use them to draw the connection between your inner upset and the upset in your body.

### Fear

Fear is perhaps the most primitive of our emotions, which may explain why it has so many offspring, including worry, anxiety, control, indecision, perfection, manipulation, hesitation, and doubt, among others. It's one of the most impactful emotions on our bodies in any form because of its capacity to shift our brains and bodies into fight-or-flight mode in an instant. It's also easy to summon. Anytime we feel uncertain due to a change in career, financial issues, or relationship struggles, we conjure up fear. Trauma, a significant life change, or an important decision can also instigate a cascade of stress hormones that won't abate until the threat is resolved.

I'd estimate that 80 percent of my clients over the years came to me suffering from pain that was a direct result of fear in some form.

Marie was one of them.

Marie was a woman in her early sixties who had a successful career in the corporate world. Her two kids were grown up, her husband of thirty years was retired, and she loved to hike, ride her bike, and, most of all, do yoga.

Marie came in with major neck pain to the point that she could barely turn her head without severe limitation. She also experienced frequent headaches and suffered from a frozen left shoulder that only had about 50 percent of its normal range of motion. She'd been suffering from her neck and shoulder symptoms for about six months, but she'd had headaches for years.

Pictures of her posture could have been on the front page of a handbook for neck pain. Her head pitched several inches forward of her shoulders, both shoulders were rounded forward, especially the right one, her right hip rotated forward, her right knee turned in, and about 60 percent of her weight was all on her left hip.

When the head moves forward of the shoulders, neck pain is almost always a forgone conclusion. As soon as her ear moved in front of her shoulder joint, all the muscles of her head and neck (up to about twenty different muscles) engaged to keep her ten-to-twelve-pound head from falling down.

Once her neck muscles engaged, the tension in her upper back all the way to the top of her skull escalated in direct proportion to the degree of displacement of her head's center of gravity. Enough tension in these muscles can constrict blood flow and oxygen to the brain, similar to wearing a tight hat all day long, making headaches and migraines common.

Due to Marie's rounded shoulder position, her shoulder joints were no longer in their ideal position for optimal motion, strength, or stability. In addition, since most of her weight was shifted onto her left hip, her shoulders no longer had a balanced base of support.

To compensate, her forward left shoulder blade locked down to help stabilize her upper body.

Full shoulder motion requires a functional, mobile shoulder blade. Without it, the range of motion in the arm bone becomes limited, creating a frozen shoulder.

Marie's posture provided a clear road map as to what needed to be addressed to eliminate her pain. But I couldn't help but wonder what was lurking underneath. I knew her frozen neck and shoulder represented something stuck inside her. I also knew that being frozen, whether in ankles, knees, hips, shoulders, or even the neck, usually represents fear—fear of having to make a difficult decision, fear of what the future will hold, fear of moving forward in a relationship or career, or some other fear perhaps deeply embedded inside from a past traumatic experience. One thing was certain: whatever her specific fear or fears, something in her life was threatening her basic human need for safety and security, and I was determined to help her bring these fears out into the light so she could face them and reclaim her peace of mind.

"Marie, would you believe me if I told you that your neck and your shoulder are frozen because of something that's frozen inside you?" I asked.

She chuckled but gave it some thought before answering. With a smile on her face, she replied, "I could believe that."

I smiled back. "Where do you think you might be currently 'stuck' in your life?"

She responded, "I'm not sure."

This is a common response. We're generally not used to diving deeper into ourselves to find answers without someone nudging us or without prior experience. I countered with a saying I use often to ease the pressure while encouraging someone to dig a bit. "If you had to guess where you may be stuck at work, home, or in your life, where would that be?"

She took a moment to answer, and I could tell she was now really considering the question. "Well, recently, I've been longing to leave my job and start a different career."

"Wow, that's fantastic! In what?"

"I really want to teach yoga."

"That's amazing!" I started, "What's stopping you?"

Again, she took time to consider the question, but now I knew we were on a roll and about to discover her underlying fear. "I've worked so hard to build my career up to this point. I'm concerned that if I leave it, I'll be throwing all that time and hard work away."

I nudged a little more. "What else?"

"I guess I'm afraid my husband won't approve."

Change of any kind can be scary, and even destabilizing, but leaving a successful career or a relationship for the unknown can lead to tremendous uncertainty and doubt. Marie's pain reflected her emotional turmoil.

According to the world-acclaimed author, speaker, and mind-and-body guru, Louise Hay, specific pains can be literal metaphors for turmoil. In her book *Heal Your Body*, she points out many of these connections, such as cancer being connected to deep resentment, symptoms like gout being related to anger, neck pain being related to fear, and so on.

Marie was consumed with fear. She was afraid to choose a new direction (neck pain) because she was concerned that she'd be throwing her career away, and she was afraid to reach out for her new dream (frozen shoulder) because her husband might disapprove. There was also a fear of the unknown: Would she even be successful at her new venture?

Finally, changing careers often means shifting a self-identity, and that can be scary and destabilizing. We often define our identities based on our jobs or careers. We say things like, "I'm a coach" or "I'm a lawyer," and it becomes part of who we are. Defending those identities is another human need that plays directly into our sense of safety and security—if we're not scientists, teachers, nurses, dads, moms, or corporate phenoms, then who are we? That's scary, no matter who you are. I experienced this when I retired from tennis. If I wasn't a tennis player or an athlete, then who was I?

Now that I understood the sources of Marie's emotional stress, it was time to help her pave a clear path toward her new goals and her new identity.

"Thanks for sharing that," I said. "Let me ask you, what are you dissatisfied with in regard to your current career?"

There was no hesitation. "I'm tired of the grind; I want more freedom in my day; I'm not feeling challenged anymore; I don't need the money at this point; I want to travel, and I really want to help people."

She listed all her reasons and motivations for shifting her life.

"Ok, and do you think your husband wants you to be happy or miserable?"

She laughed. "He's a great guy. He'd want me to be happy."

I added, "So, you have plenty of money, you're emotionally done with your old job, you're excited to live your next passion of helping others achieve optimal health, which will bring you meaningful purpose, satisfaction, and self-esteem, and your husband ultimately just wants you to be happy no matter what you do. You'll also be able to travel more, have more time to yourself, and still make money."

She nodded in affirmation to all of it. "Yes."

"And if yoga didn't work out and you absolutely needed to go back to your old job, could you?"

"I wouldn't go back, but based on my years of experience, I could easily make a good living as a consultant."

I let all that hang in the air for a moment. As she faced her concerns, she realized there was nothing to be afraid of.

That's the thing with fear; it's usually just a house of thin, unstable cards created by our minds that we make into massive, impenetrable castle walls. All it takes is a little courage and some logic to see it for what it is and to collapse the walls to rubble.

"How do you feel now about leaving your current job and embarking on a new and exciting chapter in your life?" Again, she nodded, but with tears flowing down her cheeks—the release of all that pent-up emotion.

"Thank you. I feel much better."

"I'd say you only live once, but that depends on whether you believe in reincarnation. I'll say instead that you only live once as Marie. If you stayed where you are for fear of making a change in your life, twenty years from now, what would eighty-year-old Marie think as she looked back on her life?"

"I'd feel deep regret and sadness for being too scared to follow my heart."

Case closed.

After I took her through some exercises to reset the position of her shoulder blade and bring her head back over her shoulders, I had her stand up and test her shoulder. She had gained 50 percent more range of motion already, and her pain was down significantly. We were done for the day.

I worked with Marie two more times, each time checking on her symptoms and inquiring about her life, not to provide pressure or judgment but to be an objective, nonjudgmental voice of support no matter what. As expected, Marie had spoken to her husband, and he was in full support of whatever she wanted to do. She had decided to keep ties with her old job by being a paid consultant, but on her own terms, so she still had the freedom to travel and explore her new passion. It was the best of both worlds. She also had safety, security, purpose, adventure, and connection to herself and her husband, and she didn't experience a major identity crisis. All of her needs were being met, and she was in the process of taking yoga instructor training classes.

Two weeks after her first visit, her neck and shoulder pain had decreased by 90 percent, and her range of motion in both had increased significantly. One month later, she didn't have pain in either area, and her headaches were no longer a concern.

# Meditation

Your older self or future self can serve as a powerful source of clarity and motivation.

If you're hesitant, scared, or worried about making a change in your life, or if you're struggling with a decision, try this quick and easy meditation.

Close your eyes or soften your gaze in front of you. Imagine you're in a safe space. You might be in an open field filled with beautiful flowers, near a babbling brook, on the beach watching the waves crash on the sand, or in a peaceful, remote cabin in the woods known to nobody but you. Wherever you are, bring in your eighty-year-old future self (if you're older than eighty, bring in someone much older). This future you is not only older, but much wiser from years of experience and a perspective derived from a life full of successes and failures. This you knows exactly what you did wrong and what you did right, which is why their insight is so valuable.

Ask them for their advice on what you should do about your situation. You can ask them anything about your life, including which path you should follow, which job you should take, who you can trust, and so on.

As you listen to their words, know they will always give you an answer that is both responsible and devoid of fear. Whatever their advice, look inward to see if it feels right. Thank them for their help and end the meditation.

I've used this meditation countless times, and it has always helped me shift my perspective so I could move forward after feeling stuck.

One last helpful technique to use when facing a difficult decision in your life is to ask yourself which decision points you toward growth. Which choice is the fear choice, and which is the growth choice?

You always want to move toward growth as long as you're being responsible. A growth choice is one that will lead to expanding your self-confidence, self-esteem, experience, perspective, knowledge, and self-worth, or it will challenge you in a positive way. When you make a growth choice, you're stepping into more of your potential in some area of your life. For example, if you're choosing between two jobs, you might ask yourself which one is more challenging but also more rewarding. Which one will give you more responsibility, connection, variety, and adventure, or which one might lead to something even bigger and better down the road?

A fear choice might be one you make out of fear of not being enough or fear of being let down, disappointed, or hurt. For instance, you may pass up a new job or position out of fear that you won't be able to handle the workload, the new responsibilities, or fit in with the team. Or you might be hesitant to jump into a relationship, no matter how great it seems, out of fear that they could leave you one day. Those fears all result in fear choices, and if you let them guide you, you'll never reach your true potential, nor will you ever find true happiness.

Here's another common fear choice: Many people stay in unhealthy or unfulfilling relationships because they fear being alone or they fear the unknown. Fear of the unknown is never a good reason to stay the same. All growth comes from stepping into the unknown to discover something new.

# Healing Journal

1. Are you struggling with a decision right now in your life?
2. How do you think it's affecting your body?

## Chapter 18

# ANXIETY

BARRY CAME IN complaining of chronic lower back pain on the left side of his spine just above his left pelvic bone. He also occasionally felt some sciatic nerve pain traveling down his left leg, had severe constipation at times, and suffered from an ulcer.

His posture clearly told the story of why he had back and leg pain. His left hip sat about an inch or higher above his right, the left side of his pelvis was rotated forward, and his left shoulder had fallen out of position. These imbalances were causing a concave curve of his lower spine toward his elevated hip.

Hip rotation with lateral spinal flexion is always a recipe for a vertebral disc to bulge because of the one-sided compression on the discs in the lower back. As in Barry's case, once the disc bulges, it can impinge on the sciatic nerve, sending radiating or burning pain into the leg, sometimes as far down as the foot.

One reason for his constipation was that he was breathing entirely from his chest. This was evident from his shoulders appearing constantly shrugged up toward his ears and from the lack of movement in his lower abdomen when he breathed, which meant his diaphragm wasn't expanding all the way. Anytime the diaphragm isn't able to expand and contract fully, digestion can be impeded. Involuntary muscle contraction and relaxation around the intestines, called peristalsis, is how food is moved through the small and large intestines and eventually processed as waste to be eliminated.

Normally, the abdominals should expand and contract in sync with the diaphragm, creating an on-and-off pressure differential around the stomach and intestines that helps to drive smooth muscle contraction responsible for peristalsis.

However, since Barry's diaphragm was essentially shut down and wasn't reaching its full range of motion, his abs were in a state of near-constant contraction, rendering them both less effective in aiding the digestive process.

Barry's rounded upper back and forward head posture were partly to blame for his dysfunctional diaphragm. When the thoracic back (upper back) loses its mobility, the rib cage can't completely expand, which limits both lung capacity and the amount of oxygen that's delivered to the lungs. Since full inhalation and exhalation aren't possible, the diaphragm can't reach its maximum expansion or contraction either. The other limiting factor was his emotional state. Barry was stressed to the max and full of anxiety, which led to holding his stomach in and shallow breathing, as it does for everyone.

One of the first goals of treatment when someone is experiencing any kind of pain, but especially nerve pain, is to find a position that relieves it, whether that's standing, sitting, kneeling, prone, or supine. Once the person is comfortable, we can do some work to rebalance and realign the body.

Often, when experiencing nerve referral pain or lower back pain, people feel better when lying on their back with their legs up, which is exactly what we did. I put him on his back with both his hips and knees at a ninety-degree angle.

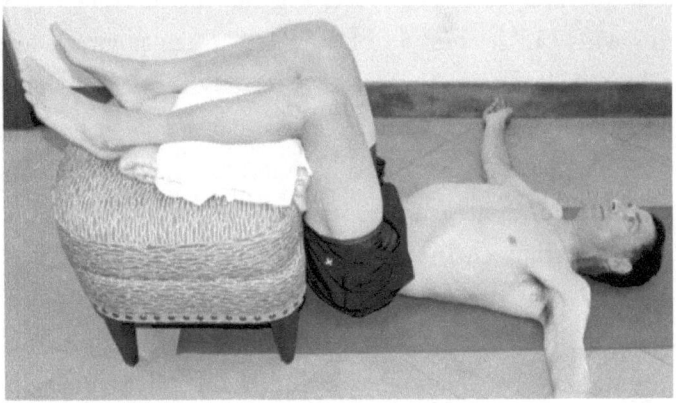

*Legs up on a chair or couch with the knees and hips as close to ninety degrees as possible*

The plan was to let his spinal muscles balance out, allow his pelvis to fall into a more neutral position, and at least temporarily relieve the pain. I also asked him to breathe by allowing his stomach to rise as he inhaled and drop as he exhaled. He needed to get his abdominals and diaphragm moving again.

Within about sixty seconds, I saw tears forming in his eyes. Based on our earlier conversation, I hadn't anticipated an emotional reaction so soon, or even at all, but I knew that whatever the reason for it, it was a necessary and positive first step. He cried for several minutes while I sat with him in silence.

Barry was allowing himself to relax, and as his muscles released their tight grip on his hips and stomach, his emotions found an escape like they'd been trapped behind a locked door that had finally been cracked open.

This is common with many people I work with and very common in this position. For many people, it's the first time in weeks, months, or even years that they're feeling their emotions.

Most of us bury our emotions to get through our day. After all, difficult emotions are problematic when you have work to do, mouths to feed, and a million other things on your plate. Plus, painful emotions aren't exactly fun to feel, which is one big reason we avoid them.

I asked if he wanted to talk about it. He courageously opened up about his life, eventually revealing his marital challenges. He loved his wife, but he didn't feel attracted to her anymore and felt tremendous guilt for it. He was also secretly seeing someone else, which compounded it even more. I was grateful for his candidness and honesty and sad for him (and his wife) that he had been holding onto so much emotional pain for so long.

Barry was stuck in the middle of his self-created turmoil and suffering and was rife with constant anxiety. For many people, anxiety is a mix of unfelt and undefined emotions that are bubbling up to the surface. For Barry, that included anger, fear, guilt, shame, and despair. Yet, instead of being acknowledged and felt, he let them linger and build.

He could end his suffering by feeling his emotions and by communicating, but there was too much fear. Barry was afraid to come clean to his wife, afraid to leave either relationship for fear of being alone, dreading the day when the truth would come out, feeling guilty for all of it, and feeling angry at both himself and his wife—none of which he would allow himself to feel.

His physical pain was a manifestation of all his unfelt emotional turmoil added to his uneven pelvis and spinal rotation.

I believe his pain also acted as a form of self-punishment because, deep down, he felt he deserved it.

All of this, in addition to his lack of diaphragm function, kept him in the fight-or-flight sympathetic nervous system response, during which his brain reflexively shut down his digestive system. Constipation resulted. He hadn't allowed himself to let go and relax for even a minute in a very long time. Adding insult to spinal injury, with all that acidic turmoil churning about in his gut, Barry began to form a sore, or many, on the lining of his stomach and intestines. They're known as stress ulcers because of their well-documented psychosomatic origins, and they can be extremely painful.

After he confided in me about his situation, I thanked him for his trust. I also pointed out that holding on to his guilt and his suffering was contributing to all his physical symptoms. He nodded immediately because he knew that they were, even if he didn't understand exactly how it worked (again, a testament to the fact we know the truth when we hear it).

I wasn't in any way judging him. I felt great compassion and empathy for Barry and his wife. He was suffering, and I knew that if he was suffering, she was as well.

When we're in pain, our loved ones suffer too, either because we've abandoned them emotionally to stew in our own emotional hell, or because they love us and don't like to see us in so much misery.

Either way, we rarely suffer alone.

Despite all this, I didn't tell Barry what to do, because I barely knew him, and it wasn't my place. Instead, I told him what I believed was causing his pain, and in telling him the truth about his posture and the effect I believed his emotions had on his pain, I presented him with a choice. He had power; he had just been refusing to use it.

He could choose to do the exercises, end the postural dysfunction, and face his emotional turmoil head-on, or he could continue on the same path of pain and misery.

Of course, his other choice was to ignore my advice and go seek someone else who would simply treat his physical pain. That would have been okay with me, too.

The exercises and breathwork I gave Barry helped him release his tight stomach muscles, shift his brainwaves into relaxation mode, and unwind his twisted spine and hips. He also needed to release the tight grip his fear and guilt had on his body, but that would mean facing the truth about his life, which was out of my purview.

When Barry got up to walk, his hips were more level, his shoulders were dropped away from his ears, and he was completely out of pain. We called it a day, and that routine became his homework for the week. The rest was up to him.

I'm happy to say that Barry did ultimately confide in his wife. Although they tried therapy, they didn't stay together. However, they parted amicably, and they remain close friends (which is a huge win).

A year later, he's happier than he has ever been, he's in love, and he's back doing all the activities he enjoys without pain. Perhaps more importantly, he's finally at peace.

It's important to recognize that when you're trapped in fear, worry, or anxiety, they are just thoughts spinning around in your head. They're not real. They haven't happened yet and may never happen.

Shakespeare alluded to the idea that a person who worries about death dies a thousand times, whereas the one who is unafraid of it dies only once. It's a great reminder that it's better to acknowledge and stay present with what's real rather than worrying about what isn't or what might be. Therefore, the first and most powerful technique to combat fear, worry, or anxiety is to confront it head-on. It's always wise to step away from the emotional rollercoaster and tap into reason to assess if the threat is real or a product of what might be or could be.

As expected, almost all worry can be quelled with some deep breathing, a little bit of logic, and a lot of reason. Then again, sometimes you have to summon the courage to investigate for yourself, as in the case of facing an uncomfortable conversation or a situation that can only be resolved through confrontation. In that case, it's often best to step up to the plate and get it done. Sometimes, that isn't possible, though, so there are several techniques to move beyond it.

It's imperative to face the monster you're imagining, so the first step is to become crystal clear on what you're afraid of. These questions will help you to clarify the objects of your fears.

# Healing Journal

1. What are your top five biggest fears right now?

Write out your top five present fears or worries. You're not writing phobias here like, "I'm afraid of snakes," you're writing current fears that are affecting your life and peace of mind right now. Writing them out helps to make them real and less scary. If you're struggling to connect to something, you might want to break it down by category to make it easier. For example, you may ask yourself what your fears are around your relationship, work, kids, parents, health, appearance, weight, happiness, success, or money.

As you write down each fear, ask yourself, is this a real or imaginary fear? Are you really going to lose your house, your relationship, or your job? Or are those things highly unlikely?

2. How many of the things you fear or worry about are out of your control?

Most of the time, you'll discover that the things you're afraid of are completely out of your control, and you need to let them go. Most political results, acts of nature, other people's actions and feelings, how quickly your body heals, and a thousand other things are completely out of the realm of what you can or should try to control.

Letting go is an art in itself, and when you learn how to do it appropriately, you'll open up a whole new world of peace and possibility. Relinquishing your attachment to controlling your world can abate so much fear, worry, and anxiety.

When you're feeling out of control, breathe deeply in and out through your nose, and imagine whatever scenario you're trying to control resolving itself in the most positive, ideal way. I do this with work projects, relationship conflicts, political elections, foreign wars, and anything else that worries me, and it's a highly effective way to abate stress of all kinds.

3. Clarify what you're afraid of and play out the worst-case scenario.

Clarifying exactly what you're afraid of forces you to look under the bed for the monster in the darkness. Maybe it isn't quite as scary as you thought, and that alone can take the sting out.

If it doesn't, you can often diffuse the energy by imagining and playing out the worst-case scenario. For example, if you're afraid of not having enough money, you might close your eyes and imagine you've lost it all. What would you do? As your mind goes into solution mode, you'll move away from fear.

You'll also find that no matter what happens, you're going to survive. You always have. You've lost relationships and money, failed tests, broken up friendships, been fired from jobs, lost loved ones, been through hell and back, and you're still here.

So, as you play out the worst-case scenario about anything, you'll conclude that it isn't ever as bad as you fear. You'll find a new job or relationship, live on after a loved one has passed, and have the resources to solve anything that comes your way.

Our brains are hardwired to find solutions, so if you play out your worst fear to its conclusion, you'll automatically come up with a plan B or C that can help to dissipate your fear.

4. Play out the best-case scenario.

Our imaginations are sometimes our worst enemies when it comes to fear, but they can also be our best allies. So, if you're caught up worrying about something that might happen in the future, you can also go back into meditation and imagine a different ending, only this time, a happy one.

Imagine finding a new job that pays you 50 percent more than what you were making before. If you fear your partner will leave you, imagine them in your mind and tell them about it. Imagine them forming a huge smile filled with love, telling you they love you unconditionally, and then wrapping their arms around you in the warmest, most heartfelt hug you've ever had. Melt in their arms and feel the love. It's impossible to feel fear when wrapped in the embrace of love.

Let your imagination work for you rather than against you.

## Meditation

This helpful meditation is about confronting the fear around your illness or ailment.

Close your eyes and focus directly on the spot of the pain or injury. If it's an illness, imagine the illness as a ball of energy sitting somewhere inside you.

Ask the spot or the illness, "What's the fear?" If it's your lower back, for example, go speak to your lower back. Imagine a ball of colored energy pulsing or throbbing at the spot, then ask that ball of energy, "What am I afraid of?" and wait for an answer. You might hear, "I'm afraid of not being good enough," "I'm afraid I'll be abandoned again," "I'm afraid of being alone," or "I'm afraid I'll make the wrong decision."

Once you receive an answer, go deeper. I refer to this as the onion process, because you're unraveling the layers of the onion until you reach the core. If you discover you're afraid of making a wrong decision, ask yourself why. What's underneath that? Are you afraid you'll be miserable and alone? And what if you are, then what? Keep following that path until you reach the end, and you'll usually discover your fear, once again, is just a construct in your brain and not worth your energy.

I did this with my right knee. One day, I tore some cartilage while playing tennis, which caused pain in one particular spot. I asked the painful spot what the fear was, and the message immediately popped into my head: I was afraid I wasn't good enough. Then, I immediately received another message: I was afraid of being a disappointment.

Two fears in one injury! Considering these were fears I had been holding onto for thirty years, I found the answer to be very valid. As I unraveled the onion, underneath all that was the fear that there was something wrong with me, leaving me alone with my shame.

The underlying root of shame is that there's something wrong with us as individuals. It's never true, but shame doesn't care; it will haunt you regardless. Once you uncover it for what it is, though, you can see it's just an illusion we choose to make very real.

Once you receive an answer as to what you're afraid of, stay with the fear. Feel it. Let the energy of that fear fill you and feel it. Don't leave it, don't dismiss it, don't question it, just feel it. Eventually, the feeling and the energy will fade. It may take two minutes, ten minutes, or more, but it will fade. If your mind wanders off, come right back to it and feel again.

Once the energy has diminished, your brain will receive the message that you're no longer afraid or under threat, and your body can relax.

### BREATHE

Breathing provides perhaps the most immediate relief from the throes of fear or anxiety and can be the most effective in the short term. After just a few targeted breaths, your body can begin to reset.

Lie on your back with your legs up or sit in a comfortable, meditative position. Close your eyes to block out any distractions, and begin to take slow, long, deep breaths. As you inhale, keep your mouth closed, feel your stomach expand, and move the breath from your lower abdomen into your chest. As you exhale, do it slowly and count out loud as you do (yes, make a sound)—one, two, three, four—until you run out of breath, then keep audibly counting. This technique is used by opera singers to expand the diaphragm, but it will also help you focus on your breath and the numbers rather than whatever's stressing you out.

You'll notice as you keep counting after you've expelled most of your air that your lower abdomen becomes involved in expelling your reserves. This is the other point of counting out loud. It allows your diaphragm to reach its full expansion, so when you take your next inhale, you'll notice a much deeper, fuller inhalation, thereby increasing the amount of oxygen intake, which will readily be gobbled up by the alveoli in the lungs and distributed to all your cells.

Remember to exhale very slowly. Ten deep breaths using this technique is all you need. Don't be alarmed if your chest begins to feel sore; that's the muscles surrounding your rib cage getting a much-needed workout.

You'll find that the more you do it, the longer you can count. The first time I tried this technique, I got to ten. After a few minutes, I was able to double it. There is no target number, though; the point is just to breathe, expand your diaphragm, and focus on the count until you don't have any more air to expel.

If you become woozy or dizzy, then stop and breathe normally until you're back to normal. Your brain and body aren't used to that much air, but over time, taking ten or more of these breaths will become easier.

# Chapter 19

## SHOCK

I REMEMBER THE day Ted "walked" through my door. He was a very fit and muscular man, about five foot nine, with short brown hair and round eyeglasses.

The word "walked" is in quotations because he took slow, short, shuffling strides like he was walking on thin ice in slippers.

Ted followed me over to a chair and very gingerly sat down. Even though we had spoken before, and I could clearly tell he was in pain, I asked him how he thought I might help.

He proceeded to tell me an unforgettable story.

A few months earlier, he had been in a foreign country doing business. When his meetings ended, he packed his bags, checked out of the hotel, and hopped into a cab with three of his colleagues on the way to the airport. A few minutes later, another driver ran a red light and T-boned them in the intersection while traveling at sixty miles an hour.

Luckily for Ted, he was sitting in the passenger seat when the other car smashed into the driver's side and was relatively unscathed. The others weren't as lucky. The cab driver and the passenger behind him were killed instantly. The other two men sitting behind Ted were severely injured, and somehow, a fire had ignited in the engine, causing smoke to fill the car. Ted was able to escape, but as he tried to help his friends, he realized they were either trapped by the wreckage or too injured to get out. Unfortunately, despite his efforts and those of the first responders, neither of them made it out before they succumbed to the smoke and their injuries. Ted said that, though he tried, he felt totally helpless to save them.

After being checked out and cleared by the medical technicians and the authorities, he took another cab back to his hotel. He said he had been feeling physically okay up to that point. However, as soon as he tried to get out of the cab, he knew something was very wrong, because he could barely move. His muscles and joints had stiffened to the point that they felt like cement. Even months later, he was still moving and walking like the Tinman from *The Wizard of Oz*, only worse.

The doctors, physical therapists, and other experts he went to apparently weren't able to help much, which was why he was sitting in front of me.

He had begun working with a psychologist for several weeks before seeing me, so it was clear he was trying to address his impairment from all angles.

The first question I asked after he relayed his terrifying event was how he felt. He began to explain his muscle tightness. Since I could already see his body was frozen, I interrupted him and clarified that I was referring to how he felt emotionally.

He acknowledged he still had nightmares. He still woke up at night thinking about the crash and the people who didn't make it out.

His response helped to explain why he was still so stiff. As he played the terrifying scene out in his head over and over, his brain still thought he was in danger, which is why it was blocking the messages to his muscles and joints to move freely.

The brain does this to all of us in a minor way when a joint is physically injured. For instance, if you sprain your ankle or knee badly enough, your brain will send the message via electrical signal and neurotransmitter to shut down some of your leg muscles.

Why? So that you don't, or can't, walk on that injured joint and damage it further. It's a primitive and automatic survival mechanism kicking in that knows your body has to heal so you can continue to hunt, gather, and survive.

Ted's brain was literally afraid to let him move. His sympathetic (fight-or-flight) nervous system was reacting as if he were still in the car, trying to set himself and the others free. He was still in shock and survival mode. He was also (understandably) still holding onto the trauma of the crash.

Ted knew he was still reeling from the trauma. He didn't need me to tell him, and this is something I find in almost everyone I work with. We know when we're emotionally compromised, upset, or holding on to grief or pain, and we know intuitively that it's affecting us physically, even if we don't consciously admit it.

This is the deeper part of our intuitive sense, our inner wisdom, that's waiting to become conscious if we only dare look. Sometimes, it takes someone to point it out to us before we make the connection between our emotional stress and our physical symptoms. Still, like pointing out to a friend of yours that they're in an abusive relationship or gently letting someone know they're drinking to avoid feeling the pain of abandonment, they already knew that on some level. I firmly believe that deep down, we often already know the truth before we hear it; we just don't always want to face it.

Ted knew he had a lot of deep emotional healing to do, but I believed if he was ever going to walk normally again, or at least in the near future, his brain had to get the message that the danger had passed and that he was now safe to move.

The goal for our session was crystal clear: Find a way to release his fight-or-flight response and then get his body moving. The first exercise was to put him on his back and get him to breathe. As he stimulated his parasympathetic nervous system and started to relax, I gently and slowly began asking his joints to move again.

Over several visits, the exercises evolved as his body slowly opened up. The more he was able to move, the more we reinforced that movement while coercing it to open up just a little further. His overall improvement was dramatic. His range of motion, ability to walk, and quality of life had significantly improved in a very short time. I lost touch with him not long after his last appointment, but I'll never forget his story or his body.

Other than working with my own body, that experience was my first major lesson in mind-and-body interconnectedness and interdependence. I learned that although the brain can hijack the rest of the body, the body can reclaim its power and similarly have sway over the mind.

Ted was the perfect example of the potential impact of shock and trauma on our bodies, and as I pointed out in an earlier chapter, we all have it to some degree, even without a plane crash.

## Healing Journal

1. Have you ever been in a state of shock?
2. What were your physical symptoms?
3. Are you still experiencing any of those symptoms?

If you are still experiencing any of the symptoms of something that created shock in the past, you might begin with the breathing exercise highlighted in the last chapter on anxiety.

## Chapter 20

# GRIEF

Stephanie came to see me some years ago, complaining of back pain on her right side. She also mentioned some painful stomach issues she had had off and on.

She was fifty-eight years old at the time, very active when she wasn't in pain, energetic, and one of those people who exuded confidence, warmth, and a bubbling personality.

We spoke briefly about her history, pain, and goals, and then I asked her, as I always do, if anything other than her back and stomach were bothering her, to which she said no.

Her posture was fairly straightforward. The right side of her pelvis was elevated and rotated, which explained why her back hurt on that side.

By the end of her first visit, the pain was gone, and I was confident she would be back to hiking, tennis, golf, and her other activities very soon.

However, when she returned for her second visit, she had made little progress, and the same was true when she returned for her third visit.

At the end of every visit, and even when she was at home, she would always feel better after doing her exercises, but the pain would return, sometimes within hours and other times within minutes.

On her third visit, instead of diving into exercises, I decided to sit her down and get to know her better. We had already spoken at length about the details of her daily life—work, kids, hobbies, passions—but I knew I was missing something. I was also confident the missing link wasn't about the exercises because she always looked and felt better after doing them.

We spoke about her parents, who were both alive and well, and her kids, who were thriving and happy. Her work was fulfilling and enjoyable, and it seemed like all was well—at least on the outside.

I had never asked about her husband before because she had told me she wasn't married, so I asked if she had ever been married before.

It turned out she had married the love of her life in her twenties, and he became the father of her two children, but he had died after a long battle with cancer several years earlier.

She had cared for him for months before his body finally succumbed. I wondered if that experience had anything to do with her stomach issues and her back pain.

I wanted to be respectful of her privacy and experience, but I also wanted to help her if she was open to it, so I gently prodded.

"Stephanie, that must have been a really horrible time for all of you. Was that the first time you've lost someone close to you?"

She shook her head and replied that her best friend, who she was very close with, died just months after her husband, this time in a car crash.

When she told me all this, you could tell she'd told the story of both of them passing many times before. It was like she was talking about someone else's life.

"Oh my gosh, that's a lot of tragedy in a short amount of time. How did you deal with it?"

She said she really didn't at the time. She had to focus on her kids, bills, work, arrangements for services, and other responsibilities.

"Were you able to take the time to grieve for them?"

"Yes, I know about all the grief work, and I've spoken with a therapist for years."

"Were you able to feel and process your grief for both your husband and your best friend separately?"

I was speaking from some personal experience. I lost my mother not long before my wife and I split up. I learned I had to grieve for my mother and my eventual divorce separately, as each had its own unique impact. I also knew that processing something like grief isn't always a one-time thing, if it's processed at all. Most people need to process it multiple times over multiple days, or even months, and going through the stages of grief means very little if they're not felt.

There's a lot of emotion inside us surrounding the loss of friends, partners, and family members—more than we know or can even consciously acknowledge. If we're feeling it, we're only capable of processing so much in one sitting before being overwhelmed.

Small bites out of that rotten apple are sometimes all we can manage, yet they are necessary in order to uncover the deeper layers underneath.

If you need to process your grief, don't suffer in silence, and know you don't have to do it alone. Grief counseling is an art in itself, and there are some wonderful professionals out there who spend their lives helping others who have experienced loss similar to yours.

Back to Stephanie. She acknowledged she hadn't really taken the time to process her husband and best friend separately. I explained that for many people, although it doesn't have to, grief can last for years and show up as physical symptoms. Stephanie was one of those people who presented herself as happy-go-lucky, together, and strong all the time. These people are always fun to be around and can form lasting, strong connections with others, but they often deeply bury their hurt, sadness, and emotional pain because those emotions don't mesh with their self-image.

They're often afraid that if they let the demons loose, they'll lose control, and they won't know how to act or who to be. They also fear they'll end up being downers and push people away.

Ironically, the very mechanism they use to stay in control—burying, ignoring, or denying their feelings—keeps them from real intimacy and from being truly connected with others.

Intimacy requires vulnerability. Vulnerability can't happen when the self-preserving protective walls never expose anything beyond what's on the surface.

I asked Stephanie if she thought her stomach issues—off-and-on pain, inability to keep certain foods down, chronic diarrhea—had anything to do with her holding on to any grief. She admitted she was sure there was still a lot inside she was holding onto, and they might be related. I encouraged her to work through her grief again, even though she thought she had already cleared it.

Stephanie came back for her fourth visit a month later. Her back pain was totally gone. She told me she had spent a lot of time processing her remaining grief and discovered she had indeed been holding on to more than she thought.

She was also back to hiking and had developed a love of pickleball with her friends. There's a lot to be said for doing the things you love with the people you love when it comes to good health.

Her stomach issues had mostly cleared up. She had also been experimenting with different foods to continue to pinpoint her particular sensitivities, so that she knew what to avoid.

She was in a good place, and I was really happy for her. It takes courage to tackle grief. It takes courage even to admit it's there and affecting your daily life.

As a side note, our guts are sensitive to even the slightest chemical changes in our bodies. Anything and everything we ingest causes a reaction. Our stomachs can tolerate an amazing amount of food stress (this reminds me of all the fast food and donuts I ate as a kid), but when our emotional chemical messengers deliver bad news repeatedly in the form of fear, anger, worry or grief, there's only so much stress it can tolerate.

As the gut becomes increasingly acidic from the continuous influx of noxious emotion and less-than-optimal food, the necessary balance between good and bad gut bacteria is thrown for a loop. It doesn't take long for our once tolerant stomachs to become upset, reflecting our upset.

It isn't uncommon for gluten, dairy, and other forms of ingestion intolerance (irritable bowel syndrome, chronic diarrhea, food sensitivity) to show up seemingly out of nowhere or come out of hibernation in the wake of an emotional incident, or from repetitive emotional setbacks.

Keep in mind that failing to heal our past keeps it present and allows it to negatively impact our future. When we don't deal with past hurt, trauma, betrayal, loss, and other painful experiences, it means we're opening the door for them to repeatedly haunt our minds and our bodies to the point that one hurtful experience turns into literally hundreds over time.

The ghosts of our past are determined to rattle their chains and remind us that they're still alive regardless of whether or not you acknowledge them. They're clamoring to be set free so they may ascend to a more serene place, just like us.

Embrace them, acknowledge them, let them speak their pain, and they'll haunt you no more.

# Healing Journal

1. Are you still grieving the loss of a loved one, the end of a relationship, or the loss of your dream job?

2. Were you excited about something in your life only to have your hopes dashed?

3. What emotions do you need to acknowledge and feel? What's stopping you from feeling them? Fear of feeling pain?

One of our biggest fears in life is the fear of feeling emotional pain. Why? Because pain hurts! Yet, feeling is healing. The loss of my mother changed my life because I allowed myself to feel a depth of sadness and loss I have never experienced before or since. Once I got to the other side of that emotional pain, I lost all my fear of feeling difficult and painful emotions, which was a fear that had been lurking in the background. It's a fear that rules most people's lives. Once you lose the fear of feeling the most difficult emotions, you will find a freedom you've never experienced before. That includes feeling grief, sadness, and loss. The key is to let yourself feel them.

## Meditation

I learned this easy and comforting meditation years ago. It has helped me and many others deal with personal loss. I believe that the people we've lost aren't really gone, they're just in a different place. We can visit them and speak to them anytime we like.

Close your eyes, put yourself in the middle of a beautiful field or in the clearing of a forest, and bring the person you've lost into the clearing with you. Hug them, hold them, feel their skin on yours, smell them, hear their voice, speak to them, tell them everything you want them to know, and let them speak to you. Their essence is still alive and within you. Stay with them as long as you like and visit them as often as you want.

This process will help you to feel like they're still in your life and a part of you, no matter how much time has passed.

## Chapter 21

# SELF-ABANDONMENT

Self-abandonment isn't an emotion, but it's born from a lack of feeling our emotions. This is a common trait for all of us. We often abandon our own needs to seek love and connection, approval, or to keep the peace. In the end, it's a recipe for mental, emotional, or even physical suffering and pain.

While traveling for work, I met a sixty-five-year-old woman at a restaurant bar where we were both having dinner. As we struck up a conversation over my delicious appetizers, she asked me what I did for a living. As is usually the case, when I tell someone that I help people heal their acute or chronic pain, they launch into all their aches and pains, struggles, all the doctors or practitioners they've seen, and either their success stories or their lack of success.

I love it and welcome it every time. Everyone has their own unique stories and journeys, and I feel blessed to have the opportunity to help them if I can. I could tell she was in pain because when she turned to talk to me, she twisted her whole body rather than just her neck.

Emily detailed her long history of neck pain and then told me that the exercises she received from the physical therapist helped, but that she rarely did them. I asked her why.

She replied that they only helped her temporarily and that she could generally tolerate the pain and get through her day. She also admitted that she blamed Hashimoto's disease for her pain. Hashimoto's is an autoimmune disorder that can lead to stiffness and pain in muscles and joints. This explained the real reason she didn't do the exercises her therapist gave her. She believed the disease was the cause of her pain, and the exercises couldn't solve that, so what was the point?

Before going into why I believed the pain was there based on her postural stress, I asked her a question. "How do you know the disease is the cause of your pain?" She admitted that she didn't.

I've worked with people suffering from Parkinson's, multiple sclerosis, fibromyalgia, chronic fatigue, rheumatoid arthritis, and countless other diseases and autoimmune disorders. The problem with blaming any disease for your pain is that you dismiss all the other potential reasons for it, like postural or emotional stress. You also render yourself powerless to change it until you cure the disease.

In my experience, when it comes to musculoskeletal pain, there's *always* an identifiable postural and emotional component that you can address, disease or not. The disease can exacerbate the symptoms because it adds systemic stress to a misaligned area that's already compromised. If you can divert the attack by solving the misalignment, you can often ease the pain.

Emily's forward head, rounded shoulders, and flat lower back spoke volumes about why she had neck and shoulder pain. Hashimoto's might have been accentuating her sensation of pain, but it definitely wasn't the root cause. Once I knew the postural contributors, I was hoping to discover a little more about the emotional ones.

During our conversation, I could tell she was very loving and caring, which piqued my curiosity. I asked, "Are you the kind of person who helps others at all costs?"

She said, "Is this normal conversation for you?"

I laughed and assured her I had a point to all these random questions a complete stranger was throwing at her. "I guess what I'm really asking is if you ever feel like you abandon yourself or your needs in order to meet the needs of others?"

She nodded. "I'm definitely that person. If somebody needs me, I jump at the opportunity to help no matter what."

She went on to describe how she left her husband years ago to live with her sister after her sister lost her husband in a fatal car crash. She helped to raise her sister's children but had eventually divorced and had been single ever since.

Dropping everything to help her sister was an admirable quality as long as the motivation was pure. In other words, loving others and doing loving things for them purely for the sake of giving is a magical and beautiful gesture. However, she abandoned her own husband and her life permanently, presumably because she felt more loved and needed in her sister's house than in her own. In the course of helping others, if the motivation is to receive love in return, then it becomes a manipulation. It becomes a trade-off that is all about the needs of the giver, not the receiver. It also comes at a steep cost. Emily had always prioritized other people's happiness and needs above her own. She subconsciously bet that if she helped someone, they would love her back, and if they loved her back, that meant she was lovable. This belief led to her abandoning her husband, her life, and her own needs to gain love and external validation of her lovability and self-worth.

The problem with this scenario is that if someone doesn't return the love or appreciation, people with this belief have to keep giving more and more, and they have to go to greater and greater lengths to find the love and validation they're seeking.

They also begin to hold deep resentment toward those who don't love them the way they think they deserve to be loved. "After all I've done for you, and you treat me like that?" It's an unwinnable scenario and a predictable cycle of both physical and emotional suffering. Resentment is a dangerous energy to be carrying around. In fact, many health professionals believe it can be the underlying emotional basis for cancer and other diseases for many.

Emily's neck pain was reflecting her postural stress and the fact that she felt everyone else's happiness and well-being was her responsibility. I believe the Hashimoto's reflected her self-abandonment. Her body was abandoning her and attacking itself just as she had abandoned herself. In my opinion, the message was to begin to love herself as much as she loved others.

Emily, bless her soul, was open to discussing all of this. She truly was amazing. I also don't believe in coincidences. I think she was looking for this conversation on some level, just as I was.

As promised, I sent her some posture exercises that would realign her hips, spine, and shoulders and relieve the pain. I also sent her a meditation to relieve anger—the same one given to me by my counselor and the same one I'll pass on to you.

She emailed me several weeks later to thank me for the exercises and the meditation. She said she was feeling much better already and that she had high hopes for a future absent of pain and struggle. I believe she'll create that future as long as she continues to do the exercises and learns to meet her own needs equally to those she loves.

# Healing Journal

1. How are you currently abandoning your needs, your body, or your health? Are you not exercising enough, drinking too much, not taking enough time for yourself, or staying in an unfulfilling job or relationship?

2. Can you correlate your symptoms to any of these forms of self-abandonment?

Blaming anything or anyone for your life or the pain you're experiencing isn't conducive to healing or happiness, even if you're completely justified in pointing the finger. If you remain a victim, you're giving away your power and remaining tied to the one who hurt you. To take your power back and give yourself a chance to heal in body, mind, and soul, ponder these questions:

3. Who or what are you blaming for your pain? Is it a

person, a disease, or an unfortunate event?

4. How can you let go of blame and take full responsibility for your recovery from here on out?

5. What does the term "take your power back" mean to you, and how might it impact your recovery?

## Chapter 22

# ANGER

MIKE HAD BEEN suffering from a cervical nerve impingement, which meant a vertebral disc in his neck had bulged and was pressing up against one of the nerves that traveled into his left arm and hand. The symptoms ranged from numbness and tingling in his fingers to excruciating pain in his arm. He also had chronic lower back pain that woke him up at night and kept him from running. Desperate to maintain his fitness, he had taken up cycling over the last several months until he began to feel nerve pain in his arm after every long ride.

Mike was fifty-five and single with two kids who split their time between parents. He was a successful architect but felt burned out and longed for the day he could get away from it all. He loved his kids dearly but felt trapped amid the daily grind of going to work and caring for them, only to wake up and do it all over again the next day. He called his daily routine, coupled with nearly constant pain, his "personal Groundhog Day," referring to the 1993 Bill Murray movie, *Groundhog Day*, about a man who is forced to relive the same day over and over again.

Mike's posture was straightforward and typical of someone with low back pain. His upper back and shoulders were rounded forward and stuck, while his lower back remained neutral. This meant his upper and lower back muscles were engaged in a tug-of-war. His upper back was trying to collapse his upper body forward, forcing his lower back to pull the opposite way to hold him up. When he interlaced his hands behind his head and pulled his elbows back, his elbows barely moved, indicating severe tightness in his upper back and shoulders.

When he bent over to touch his toes, it wasn't a pretty sight either. He barely reached past his knees, indicating his lower back muscles were like immovable steel cables.

Mike's rounded upper back also caused his head to shift forward, nearly doubling the pressure on the muscles and vertebrae of his neck. Cycling made everything worse, because he had to lean forward to grab the handlebars, which forced him to look up so he could watch the road. This compressed his neck and the bulging disc even more.

**Cervical Extension and Compression**

*The streamlined position forces extension in the neck. It's normal, but some can suffer if there's also a twist in the neck at the same time.*

Mike's right shoulder was also lower than his left, creating more stress on one side of his neck. You can mimic his posture by rounding your upper back forward, continuing to look straight ahead, and then dropping one shoulder to make it lower than the other. You'll notice more tension on one side of your neck.

Cervical disc herniations almost always occur from a twist

in the neck that emanates from rounded, imbalanced shoulders. Unfortunately, most doctors and therapists miss the underlying scapular imbalance and only treat the neck pain with medication and neck exercises, or worse, they fuse the vertebrae of the neck.

His neck wasn't the problem. His rounded upper back (postural stress) combined with some significant emotional turmoil were, though. In my experience, nerve pain anywhere in the body is often a sign of anger in some form, whether it's rage, resentment, irritation, bitterness, frustration, or another closely related cousin.

Mike was full of rage. Rage emerges when you have anger about a person or a situation you feel powerless to change. Mike felt powerless to change his work situation or his home life. He was burnt out but couldn't afford to retire due to monthly alimony payments on top of his mortgage, and he couldn't travel for long because of his obligation to his ex-wife and kids. He also felt powerless to change his pain, which had been going on for months in his arm and years in his lower back. He couldn't even exercise, making his emotional state even worse.

Once I took pictures of him so he could see his misalignment and explained the concept of postural and emotional stress, he seemed to breathe a sigh of relief. He had no idea his back and arm pain were connected, not to mention how his emotional stress exacerbated his symptoms. He said he felt hope for the first time in years.

When someone can actually see the evidence of their misalignment and connect it to their pain, they're able to imagine a pathway to healing. For many people, after years of searching for answers, this means feeling a sense of relief and hope that their situation can change and that they can return to their previous lives free of pain.

Mike was able to change his posture and relieve the strain on his neck. Once the curve in his upper back began to move in the right direction, the pain in his lower back also began to abate. Although Mike's work and home life were going to take time to change, he was able to relieve his anger through meditation and some anger work.

As he addressed his pain from both angles, his arm pain disappeared after only a week. The back pain he'd been carrying for years also disappeared completely within a few weeks.

The amazing thing about addressing the root cause of any problem is that it usually doesn't take long for the symptoms to improve. Almost everyone I work with is initially shocked they feel better so quickly after having spent months or years searching for a solution. It doesn't always happen that quickly for everybody, but if you're addressing the root cause, it's only a matter of time before things begin to improve.

# Healing Journal

1. What are you angry about presently?

Write everything that comes to mind and feel your anger presently and thoroughly. The key here is to really let it in and stay with the feeling until it fades and disappears. This is an easy and effective technique for clearing present anger before it gets buried in a wrist or an ankle or rears its ugly head somewhere in your life.

Perhaps a current conflict (or several) in your life is causing you a great deal of angst, such as a difficult child, an irritating coworker, a fight with your spouse, or an issue with a parent.

Whatever the source, feel your anger. Feel it some more and then more until there's no more left to feel. Then feel it some more.

Eventually, you will have nothing left, or you will just feel emotionally spent. That's when you know you've drained the energy out of the emotion.

Oftentimes, once you push past the anger, the feeling will transform into something much more constructive, like acceptance, sadness, hurt, compassion, or even forgiveness. Just let in whatever comes up. Sit with it without judgment. Simply feel.

When you're finished, you might say, wow, that was a lot! Yes, and congratulations. You're no longer being held prisoner by an energy that isn't serving you.

2. Where do you feel the anger in your body?

When you close your eyes and feel your anger, where do you notice it in your body? Is it in your chest, your stomach, your head, your back, or somewhere else you didn't expect? Get in touch with where you're feeling it, then imagine that sensation as a ball of energy. Give it a color, a size, and a shape. Is it a bright color, or is it dull? Is it shining, intense, and pulsing, or dull and lifeless? Is it round and small, or gigantic with sharp edges? Once you've given it a form and defining characteristics, breathe deeply and imagine it getting smaller, less bright, and less intense. Let the color change and become more muted. With every breath, continue to shrink it down until you barely know it's there. This is a powerful way to diffuse your anger purposely and consciously.

This is another effective technique for relieving pain or illness. Give it a color, shape, size, etc., then change it to something smaller, less threatening, and lifeless. You'll be surprised at how much it can help.

3. How could your unresolved anger be related to your painful condition?

Even if you don't believe it is, step outside yourself and ask: If my anger was related to my current physical pain, where would the source of that anger be?

Speak to the pain in your body. Ask it, "What are you angry at," or "Who are you angry at?" You might receive a vision or words in your head that point to the source of your anger. Maybe it's a parent, your spouse, a former boss, or a close friend who did something to upset you.

When you pinpoint the source, which is usually a person or sometimes a situation, you need to take several minutes and feel your anger. Don't rationalize it or make excuses for it; just close your eyes, put yourself in the feeling, and feel it all the way through until it's gone or greatly diminished.

There are many different offshoots of anger, including rage, resentment, hate, frustration, hostility, and more. Each emotion has its own qualities that usually blend a mix of emotions. For instance, rage is often anger mixed with a feeling of powerlessness, and resentment can be anger at being treated unfairly or unjustly. As you process your anger, some of these other emotions, including powerlessness or a feeling of injustice, might arise, in which case, stick with that particular emotion until it passes as well.

## The Anger Letter

I want to introduce you to the anger letter. The anger letter is one of the most effective techniques you will ever use to purge and release anger from all parts and times of your life. I first learned it from my counselor, Chris Andersonn, as it was passed down to him by his mentor, but there are different versions of the anger letter throughout the psychology world. Use this technique to release anything you're angry about in your life, including your pain, a frustrating situation, a past event, a hurtful person, or anything that comes to mind.

You can write it to a specific person, or you can make it more general. If it's to a person, you start as you would any letter with, "Dear [Person]," Then write everything you're angry about. "I'm furious that you abandoned us and left us to fend for ourselves," "I'm angry you don't seem to care about me," "I'm angry you dismissed me so easily," etc. You can write things like, "I'm angry you never make your bed," "I'm angry you interrupt me when I'm speaking," and so on.

Don't be concerned about spelling, punctuation, or grammar; just write and let it flow out of you. Let yourself be immersed in the anger and the writing and keep writing everything that comes to mind. Really feel the emotion, though. You can write this to a parent, a friend, a significant other, a boss, an aunt or uncle, or to whomever you pinpoint as the source of your anger. You're not going to send it; this is only for you.

If you're focused on a particular person, write out everything they've done, said, or implied that has angered you. Include everything that comes to mind, no matter how large or how insignificant it may seem logically. Logic is not part of this exercise; the feeling is the exercise, and it's the only thing that matters.

When you have nothing left to say, the charge of the emotion is diminished, and you can fold up the letter and hide it away. Come back the next day and read it word for word. Once you've read through it, at the end of what you've written, add to it whatever comes up, feeling the anger and staying present with it. You'll notice deeper layers of anger begin to surface. Again, write until there's nothing left to say. When you're finished, fold it up again and hide it for a second time.

On the third day, you'll read it again word for word, take all the time you need to add to it and sign your name. Don't add a salutation; just sign your name. Then burn it.

One word of caution: Don't protect anyone from your wrath. It will be easy to hold back because you're feeling like you're betraying someone for saying all these things behind their back, or because you'll feel guilty for being "mean."

You're not betraying them at all. Instead, you're honoring the impact they've had on your life, and you're being responsible for your own feelings. This is about you and you alone, not them, and by writing all of your anger, you're not blaming them; you're feeling your feelings. They're never going to see it, anyway.

If you're not writing to a specific person, you can address your letter, "To whom it may concern," and use the same technique, but write out anything and everything you're angry about. "I'm angry John didn't return my text," I'm angry my mother keeps hounding me to call her," "I'm angry I lost my job for no reason," I'm angry my fifth-grade teacher kicked me out of class and embarrassed me in front of the other kids," "I'm angry my sister ruined my favorite sweater." Whatever pops into your head from the past or present, put it down without filtering it or sugarcoating it.

Don't try to be nice, proper, respectful, or perfect; just write with raw emotion and strength and get everything out. You may write for ten, twenty, or thirty minutes or more, but stick with it for as long as it takes to purge the emotion.

I've written ten pages of anger before, so there's no such thing as too much.

I like to say: elaborate, extrapolate, and expectorate. Spit it all up and get it all out.

Burning it after the third day symbolizes that you've purged your anger, you're done with the toxicity, and you're moving on with your life. If you can't burn it, don't worry; tear it up or shred it and then flush it down the toilet. Don't leave it in your house, though; you don't want that energy in your space.

Afterward, I recommend heading out for a walk and spending a few minutes to fill yourself with gratitude to replace the anger you just purged. It will also feel good to shift gears.

Make sure to save some of that gratitude for yourself to honor and recognize your vulnerability and honesty and for taking a major step toward more freedom in every aspect of your life.

Return to this technique anytime you find the need to purge your anger. These tools have been serving me for thirty years, and they'll serve you for the next thirty years, too.

If you're really upset about something in the present, just stop for a second, close your eyes, and feel the anger that comes up for you until the energy is gone. It might take a few minutes, but when you deal with it right away, there shouldn't be too much to release.

This is one way to feel your emotions presently as they happen. If something upsets you, close your eyes and feel. Keep feeling until the feeling is gone. It's only energy, after all.

## Chapter 23

# HURT

Though they're different emotions, anger and hurt often intertwine. Hurt can transform into anger, as is the case when someone physically punches you in the arm, and after taking a second to soothe the pain, you punch them back harder. In this case and many others, hurt reminds us that we're vulnerable, and to cover up that vulnerability and reclaim our power, we revert to anger. Yet, hurt refers to an experience of pain, whereas anger is more of a reflexive and aggressive response.

There are other important distinctions between the two as well. Where anger can be felt and released immediately and be gone a moment later, hurt can leave a wound. If left unhealed, that wound can turn into a scar that can damage you emotionally and physically in the future.

Anger also has a timestamp. It can diminish or even disappear as time passes, but a big enough hurt can withstand the test of time. In fact, if you speak to someone about a past hurtful experience, they'll often talk about it as if they're feeling it in the present moment. That's because they are. They're reliving it all over again as if it's happening to them right then and there, even if the event was decades earlier.

Emotional or psychological hurt can also be significantly more damaging than anger when it's personally directed at you, especially if someone has made you feel devalued.

This is the reason it's important to heal the hurt underneath the anger. Anger is often the mask covering the wound, but releasing it isn't enough to heal what's underneath.

This brings us to a woman I worked with some years ago, who I'll call Jane. She experienced constant neck and jaw pain for years. In fact, she was limited in how much she could open her mouth. She even commented that she noticed her voice wavered and sounded soft when she spoke. She's not the first person I've worked with who had these exact symptoms.

From a postural perspective, I could see her head sitting forward of her shoulders, which is always the first clue as to why her neck and jaw hurt. As her head moved forward of her shoulders and out of alignment, her neck and jaw muscles were being recruited to hold her head up. The farther her head jutted forward, the more taught it pulled the muscles on the front of her neck, which at some point began to constrict her vocal cords.

The postural solution was obvious, which was to realign her head over her shoulders. The emotional component was obvious to me, too, but she hadn't correlated her past emotional pain to her physical pain yet. Hardly anybody ever does until it's pointed out to them, and even then, most people shrug it off as a coincidence.

To help her connect to her inner pain, I asked when she first felt she had lost her voice (and her power) in her life. I wasn't asking it from a physical sense; I was asking about the point where she first felt insignificant, stifled, small, and invisible, which are all hallmarks of feeling devalued and hurt.

She said she felt that way from a young age and immediately recalled an experience when her mother told her she was too loud and obnoxious. Good little girls were to be nice and keep quiet.

That sounded hurtful, to say the least. When we're little, we think our parents know everything, so when they tell us we're flawed, we tend to believe it.

From that day forward, she played out that belief (and her hurt) as if it were a sacred law. At home, she was the wife who never complained and did all the things she believed a wife and mother were supposed to do; at work, she remained silent, as men underneath her earned promotions and treated her like she wasn't their equal. All that time, she held her voice, and all that time, she built up years of rage and anger around her hurt.

I asked her how hurtful it felt to be told by someone she loved and trusted that she was too loud and obnoxious. Then, I asked how it felt to be ignored at home, passed up for promotions, and devalued at work, and she began to cry.

I wasn't trying to stick it to her; I was simply trying to give her a glimpse into what she'd been suppressing for over forty years. She had never acknowledged the depth of her pain before. She had never felt her hurt until now, and it was finally being released in the form of healthy, flowing tears.

I asked her if she was ready to reclaim her power and transcend the hurt she received from her mother, to which she replied, "Absolutely." Since it all seemed to have begun with her mother's cold and cruel words, I had her take a few deep breaths, close her eyes, and go back to that moment in her mind. I told her to walk right up to that little girl who was vulnerable and confused, lift her up, and wrap her in her adult arms. Then, I asked her to tell that little girl, with every ounce of honesty and unconditional love, that she isn't loud or obnoxious at all but wonderful, fun, beautiful, and absolutely perfect just the way she is. I told her to tell the girl she would take it from there; she didn't need to worry; she could go be a kid and have fun and be as loud as she wanted to be. There was nothing wrong with her, and there never was.

Finally, I guided her on how to regain her power. I advised her (as her adult self) to confront her mother in meditation immediately after the moment her mother shamed her when she was a child, and to tell her mother never to speak to her child that way again. When I asked what her mother's reaction was, she said she just nodded in agreement and apologized.

I encouraged her to say anything else she wanted to say to her mother right then in meditation. She took several minutes and then opened her eyes. I asked how she felt.

"Really, really good," she said with a clear, calm, and bold voice. I pointed out how much more even and clear her voice was all of a sudden, and she grinned from ear to ear.

I let her know she could repeat that same technique with her former husband, her coworkers, her bosses, and anyone else if she wanted. I also suggested she write an anger letter, because she had bottled up so much anger over her lifetime that it, too, needed to be released.

Loving and reassuring your inner child and confronting the person who hurt you in meditation are powerful and effective ways to reclaim your power and begin to heal past or present hurt.

## Healing Journal

1. Similar to Jane, could your current physical symptoms be reflecting your past or present hurt?

2. When you feel emotionally hurt, do your symptoms increase?

3. When you recount the hurt you received, does it feel dull and achy in your body, does it drain you of energy, or does it feel sharp and intense?

4. Do your physical symptoms play out the same way in your body?

These questions are simply an exercise in awareness. When you can connect your physical symptoms to your past or present emotional pain, a light can illuminate inside you, and your fear about the roots of your pain can dissipate.

As you uncover your hurt, if it feels overwhelming, I encourage you to enlist the help of a trusted counselor for support and further healing. I also suggest going into meditation and speaking to your child, your adolescent, or young adult to understand their fears, hurt, anger, or any other emotion that might be holding them, or you, back. After you speak with them, embrace them and love them. Their pain is almost always the result of a separation from love, as is yours.

# Part IV
*A Pathway to Healing*

## Chapter 24

# TIME TO ALIGN

Now that you've begun the important and rewarding work of healing some of your emotions and the emotional energies that may have been blocking your body's ability to heal, it's time to address the other potential blockage—postural stress. First, though, I want to tell you a relevant story to illuminate your path.

Several years ago, I was walking through my former clinic in San Francisco and one of my therapists asked if I could take a look at a client he was working with. She had low back pain. From a posture perspective, her hips were swayed way forward of her ankles and shoulders, which put all the strain and the load of gravity on her lower back. Imagine going into a standing backbend and holding it for years, and that's how she looked and felt. Her shoulders were also rounded forward, and her head had moved forward to follow her center of gravity (the head always follows the hips, with a few painful exceptions). The therapist had given her all kinds of exercises to address her rounded shoulders and forward head, but nothing was helping.

Upon looking at her, I immediately understood why. He wasn't addressing her body as one interconnected and intertwined unit. Instead, he was too focused on the pieces and parts. So, I asked her to bend over to touch her toes without bending her knees. After a minute, she came up with nearly perfect posture—no more rounded upper back or forward head, and her hips lined up directly under her shoulders. The fifteen exercises she had done before hadn't moved the needle an inch, whereas one move changed everything in an instant. How and why that worked is for another time, but suffice it to say, it restored balance to all the right places.

I recount this story because you're about to take the first steps toward solving your postural and mechanical stress. I also want to drive home the fact that impacting that stress can be immediate, and therefore, so can symptom relief. But it can also take several weeks or months, depending on your body, beliefs, dedication, and type of pain.

It's true that some people and bodies are more malleable than others, but like neglected buildings, with the right tools and dedication, even the most hopeless structures can be beautifully restored.

If you're still not sure specifically how your pain is tied to your posture, don't worry. You don't have to know exactly how it's connected to heal it any more than you need to know how a muscle works to heal a tear. You do have to know that postural stress is a reliable predictor of pain, so it behooves you to tackle it.

If you did the self-assessment in the chapter "Discovering Your Imbalances," then hopefully, you've discovered your own misalignments, including any type of shoulder rounding, one shoulder that's lower, one foot that turns out more as you stand and walk, the inability to touch your toes as you bend over, and more. You're going to use your assessment to determine the sequence that's right for you.

If you didn't do the assessment, no problem; we can still be friends. Common symptoms are listed with each specific postural imbalance, so you can choose the sequence that most closely fits your symptoms and correlates to the posture you think most closely resembles you.

Thankfully, you don't have to address each individual imbalance separately. Every part is connected to every other body part in one way or another, so we can address them collectively. We'll do this with four separate routines plus a sequence to address current, acute pain. Combined, these exercises and sequences are specifically and carefully designed to address every postural dysfunction you discovered in your assessment, plus all the ones you're still blissfully unaware of.

"But David," I can already hear you saying, "I've been in pain for years, visited five different doctors and surgeons, worked with countless physical therapists, massage therapists, trainers, and bodyworkers, and I still have pain. How can you expect me to find relief in a few exercises that don't even look that difficult?"

You can experience relief the same way the lady who touched her toes did. She had back pain for decades, had seen every pain expert on the planet, and was out of pain permanently in two weeks after doing one exercise every day. She isn't the only one, either. This happens all the time with these exercises.

If she can solve her pain with one exercise after decades of agony, you can solve yours, too. The key is to pinpoint the right sequence, which is why I'm giving you four to choose from. How did I come up with these sequences? After over twenty years and having worked with thousands of clients, I've pinpointed specific common postural imbalances in everyone that I estimate are responsible for 80 to 90 percent of all musculoskeletal aches and pains, especially when combined with emotional stress. Here are the four postural and mechanical imbalances:

1. Rounded shoulders coupled with upper back tightness
2. Pelvic (hips) and scapular (shoulder blades) disparities
3. Swayed forward hips
4. Improper hip and spinal mechanics

Most people are a combination of all four, but one condition usually predominates. To be clear, the sequences aren't addressing pain. They address the imbalances and joint dysfunctions behind it. Therefore, you have to be willing to leave your training behind.

Like everyone else who has been through the American model of pain treatment (and like all the experts within it), you've been trained:

- To treat the symptom rather than the body as a whole
- To believe you're in pain because the area is weak, so it needs to be strengthened
- To believe you need to strengthen your core

- To believe you have to stretch
- To believe the more difficult the exercise, the more beneficial it is

If you're nodding your head, let me point out that this antiquated way of treating chronic pain leaves over 50 million Americans a year still dealing with it, including, and presumably, you.

You need to drop your preconceived notions and expectations driven by past experience and be ready for the fact that although some of these exercises may not look impressive, they're powerful, effective, and proven to work.

If you give in to the process, pay close attention to your body, respond to what's working and what isn't, do the exercises in order, follow the form closely, and are willing to dedicate about ten to twenty minutes each day, then I believe you'll discover a significant improvement in your pain. If, for whatever reason, you don't, or your symptom is more emotionally driven, then continue to address the emotional energies and blockages that contribute to the pain by completing the healing journal questions and meditations.

Common pain symptoms of each particular postural imbalance are listed, along with any potential contraindications, which are exercises or sequences you should avoid if you have particular symptoms or medical conditions. Nothing beats tuning into your body, though, so if something hurts or doesn't feel right, skip it and move on to the next exercise or sequence.

## #1: ACUTE PAIN SEQUENCE

Start here if you're in a great deal of pain or your body just needs to take it easy. Beware, though, this sequence will undoubtedly deceive you. While the exercises look easy, they're incredibly powerful and impactful. In fact, they've been effective at relieving postural stress and pain of all kinds for thousands of people I've worked with over the last twenty years and counting.

Don't get me wrong, nothing works for everyone, but this sequence might be the one that saves the day if you're experiencing something acute.

The only caveat is that two out of the three take time, but trust me, they'll be well worth the time investment and more. In fact, I recommend doing these exercises throughout your life just to reset, relax, and rebalance.

Keep in mind that acute pain is most often the result of a postural and mechanical imbalance coupled with some sort of present emotional turmoil. You should address both to cover your bases and to honor the mind-and-body connection. Therefore, after this sequence, I'm going to present a quick meditation you can do to clear some of the emotional energy. The meditation can be done while you're doing the exercises, too, so it doesn't add any time to the routine. This sequence, above all others, will also shift your nervous system into the rest-and-digest mode and out of the fight-or-flight mode, so if you're particularly stressed emotionally or have been on the go, this is also a great place to start.

**Symptoms Addressed**: All symptoms, including nerve pain in the lower body, lower, mid, and upper back pain, hip pain, shoulder pain, digestive issues, degenerative hips, and fibromyalgia.

**Contraindications**: Avoid any exercises that increase pain anywhere. If you have a rotator cuff tear, skip the pullovers and the modified floor block.

If you have radiating nerve pain from your neck into your arms or hands, or if your neck is uncomfortable, put a small pillow under your head while lying on your back for the specified times.

**Sequence:** Do the exercises in the order they appear and pay close attention to your form.

## Static Resting Position: 5 Minutes

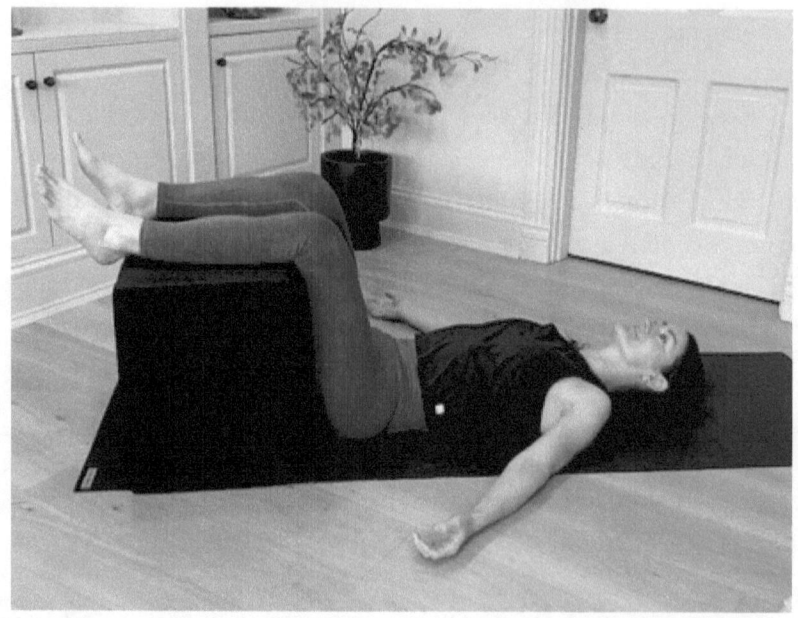

Lie on your back with your knees and hips at ninety degrees and your knees resting on a chair or couch. Your palms should be up and your arms out to your sides below your shoulders. Relax your neck, lower back, and hips. Let the ground support you. There should be no muscle tension anywhere in your body. Breathe deeply in and out through your nose. This exercise realigns the entire spine, balances out the muscles that surround the spine, and enables the back muscles to relax.

## Knee Squeezes with a Pillow: 40 Repetitions

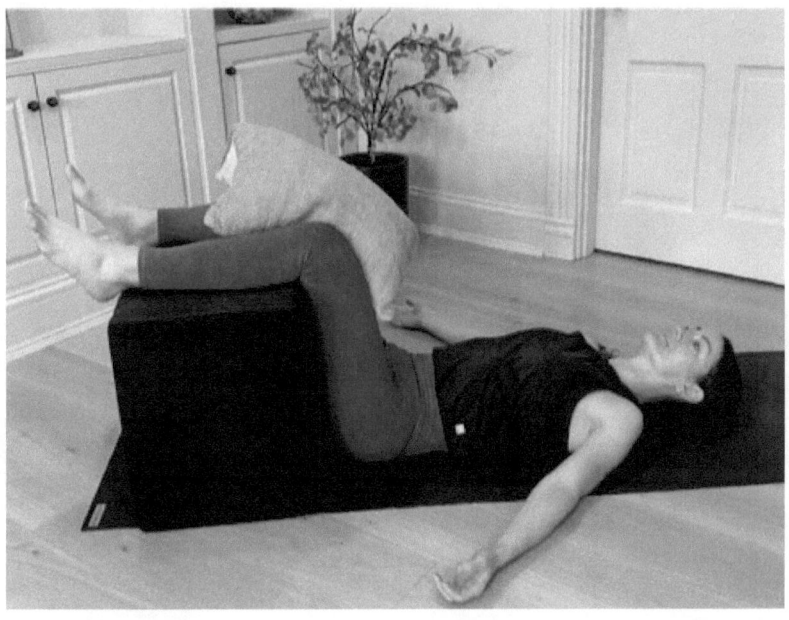

Place a pillow from your bed or couch (or a yoga block) between your knees and squeeze and release for the desired repetitions. Try to keep an even pace (not too fast or slow) and focus on the inner thighs doing equal work. Relax your shoulders and neck. This exercise reminds the hip muscles of their jobs while asking the lower back muscles to relax.

## ARM PULLOVERS:
## 30 REPETITIONS

Interlace your fingers and palms together and straighten out your elbows with your arms pointed straight up toward the ceiling. Relax your shoulders and neck. With your elbows straight, draw your hands up over your head toward the floor. Try to touch the floor with your thumbs if you can. If not, go as far as is comfortable without bending your elbows. Bring arms back and forth from the front of your chest to as far over your head as you can reach. The pace should be slow and smooth. This exercise restores motion to the shoulder joints, realigns your mid and upper back, and enables the lower back muscles to relax. Don't arch your back while doing this exercise. Keep it relaxed.

## ELEVATED HIP TRACTION: 10 MINUTES

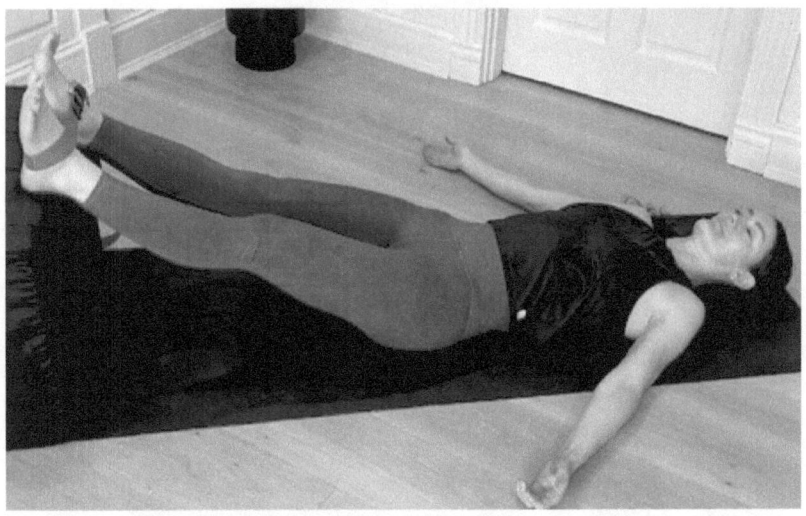

Place your heels on the edge of a chair or couch. Tie a yoga strap or belt around your feet with your feet no wider than fist-width apart. Relax your feet out on the strap. It's there to hold your feet straight with your toes pointing straight up toward the ceiling so you don't have to hold them yourself. Scoot away from your heels until your legs are completely straight. Relax your upper body and your legs completely and breathe deeply in and out through your nose. This exercise relaxes and rebalances your hip muscles and your spinal muscles. It also helps to restore proper alignment of the ankle, knee, hip, and spine.

## PRONE CHEST STRETCH: 5 MINUTES

Place each elbow on a pillow, shoeboxes, or a stack of books of equal height. They should be straight out from your shoulder, and your elbows should be bent at ninety degrees. Rest your elbow and forearm on the pillow. The pillows should be zero to eight inches high, depending on your comfort level. The higher the pillow, the more stretch on the shoulder and chest muscles, so choose the best height for your comfort. Extend your legs behind you, touching big toes together and allowing the heels to separate. Relax the legs. Let your forehead rest on the floor.

You should feel taller and more relaxed after this sequence, almost like you've had a great massage.

## Meditation

Since you have some time when lying on your back, I recommend this easy meditation. It helps to close your eyes to tune out any distractions, but it's not necessary if that's uncomfortable for you. Begin by taking five deep breaths in and out through your nose to relax. Try to let your stomach rise as you inhale and fall as you exhale. Now, in meditation, ask yourself:

What in your life is creating current emotional turmoil or stress?

What emotions are coming up for you when you think of this turmoil (anger, rage, hurt, worry, anxiety, depression, etc.)?

You might be feeling a combination of several emotions, but try to tune into the strongest one. Once you know the dominant emotion, focus on it and feel it. If it's anger, feel your anger. Let it in and feel the energy without editing it, and without judgment or inhibition. The same goes for fear, hurt, or any other emotion. Remember, hurt is something someone has done that you've taken personally or has made you feel devalued. It is its own emotion, even though it often shifts to anger.

Feel the emotion until the energy and intensity fade and even disappear. It might take five minutes or fifteen. When finished, open your eyes or bring your focus back to the present moment. With deep conviction and enthusiasm, I can tell you that when you learn to feel your emotions in this way—by bringing them into your awareness and feeling them to completion—you will have learned a powerful tool that will support your physical, mental, and emotional health throughout your life.

I recommend using this meditation in conjunction with all of the following sequences, and for any pain you're experiencing now or in the future.

## #2: ROUNDED UPPER BACK AND SHOULDERS

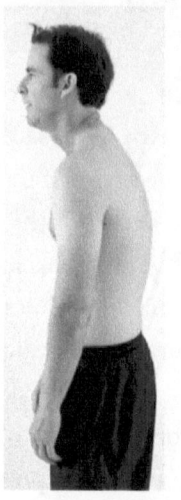 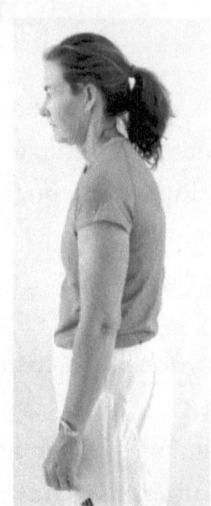

*Notice the slumped and rounded shoulders and extended necks on both examples.*

Rounded, forward shoulders, a rounded upper back, or a combination of the two are the most common forms of postural stress. They are also easy to spot and improve and are the most common contributor to pain and symptoms in all areas of the body, because they disconnect the spine from itself. Allow me to explain what I mean by "disconnect."

The spine is designed to move as a unit. When you bend over to touch your toes, each vertebra of your lower back should move, followed by those in your mid and upper back. The same is true when you bend backward but in the reverse direction. For each of the four major motions of the spine—rotation, flexion (forward bend), extension (backward bend), and lateral flexion (side bend)—each segment of the spine is supposed to move with the other one above and below it to produce fluid motion.

When your upper back is rounded forward, and especially when your shoulders or upper back are stiff and lack full mobility, the spine moves in pieces and parts rather than together. Those pieces and parts that move at least get a break, but the parts that don't move never have an opportunity to relieve the built-up tension. It would be like sitting in a car all day long without stretching your legs. They would become stiff and potentially painful. That's your spine when any part of it isn't fully functional and able to move congruously with its cohorts.

A lack of fluid motion isn't the only problem with this posture, though. When the shoulders round forward or kyphosis sets in, the load on the spine changes as well. When the spine changes position from an S-shape to an exaggerated S-shape, or even a C-curve (see pictures below), some parts of the spine take more weight and stress than the other parts. This is especially true for the neck and the lower back, which is why painful symptoms and conditions like degenerative disc disease, spondylolisthesis, disc herniations, stenosis, and arthritis are so common in these areas.

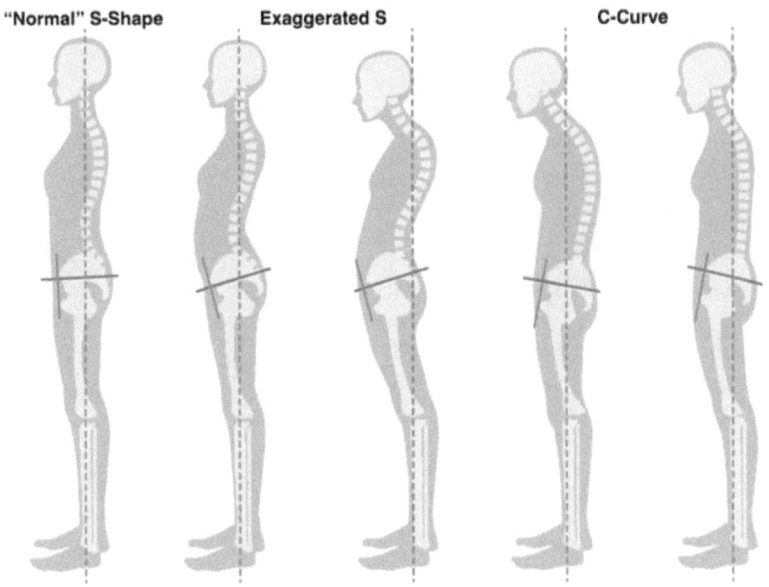

*Different degrees of spinal curve from a "normal" S-curve to a flat spine that resembles a C.*

Doctors often try to fix these conditions with surgery or exercises to strengthen the muscles of the spine. Strength isn't the problem, though. The issue is the posture. As you restore that, strength and muscle balance will follow.

**Symptoms:** Neck pain, headaches, migraines, TMJ, upper shoulder and upper trapezius tension, upper, mid, and low back pain, shoulder, wrist, and elbow pain, degenerative disc disease, spondylolisthesis, stenosis, breathing difficulties, gastrointestinal issues, brain fog, slow digestion.

**Contraindications:** Don't do this routine if you have pain during any exercise, a spinal disc bulge or herniation, sciatic nerve pain or nerve pain in the legs, or drop foot.

**Sequence:** Do the exercises in the order listed and always pay close attention to form.

## Kneeling Shoulder and Chest Stretch: 1 Minute

While on your knees, place your elbows on the seat of a chair or couch with your elbows bent ninety degrees and hands resting on your forearms. Rest your forehead on the chair and walk your knees back until they're directly underneath your hips. Let your chest and stomach relax and drop toward the ground. You might feel a stretch in your chest, your shoulders, or both. Relax your spine and let your lower back form an arch. This exercise repositions the mid and upper back, releases the tight muscles in your chest, stomach, and underarms, and reconnects the spinal muscles from top to bottom.

## SUPINE UPPER SPINAL TWIST: 1 MINUTE, EACH SIDE

Lie on one side with your knees and hips at ninety degrees. Your knees and ankles should be stacked on top of each other. Without letting your knees come apart or the top knee slide off the bottom knee, open your top arm up and over toward the opposite side with your palm facing up toward the ceiling. Let your head relax on the ground. If needed, you can place a pillow under your head to keep your neck comfortable. Breathe deeply in and out through your nose and allow your mid and upper back to relax. You might feel a stretch across your chest, on your sides, or in your back. This exercise restores motion and function to the spine while opening up the chest and realigning your upper back. Repeat on the other side.

## CATS AND DOGS:
## 10 TIMES IN EACH DIRECTION

With your hands under your shoulders and knees under your hips, round your spine up toward the ceiling as far as possible with your head down, then roll your spine the opposite way. As your back arches (picture on the right), allow your shoulder blades to drop together and look up toward the ceiling.

## WALL HAMSTRING STRETCH: 3 MINUTES

Lie on your back with both legs up on the wall. Push your knees toward the wall, tighten your thigh muscles, and flex your feet back toward your knees. Keep your feet straight rather than turned out. Your tailbone should be on the ground, and your arms should be out to your sides with your palms up. You should have your knees locked out, so scoot as close to the wall as is comfortable while keeping your legs completely straight. You should feel a light to medium stretch in the back of your legs. Scoot further away from the wall to decrease the stretch if the stretch is too intense. This exercise repositions the hips and rebalances the muscles of the spine. You'll also get a nice stretch in the back of your legs!

## WALL SIT: 1 MINUTE

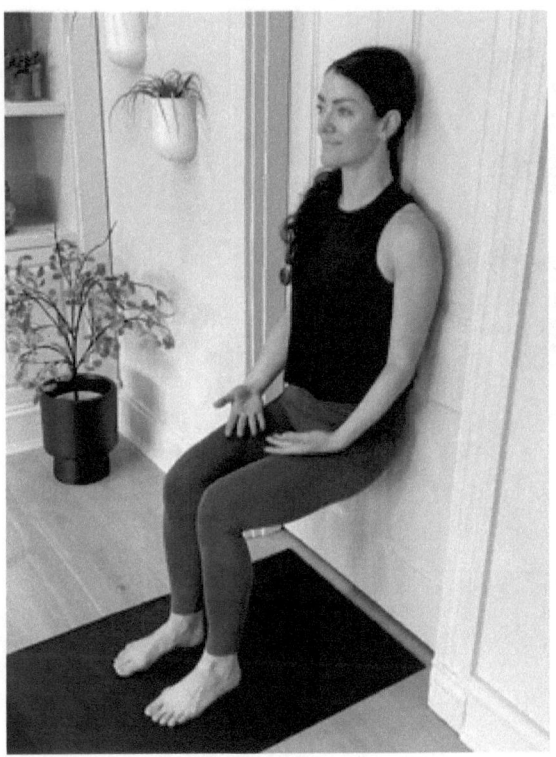

Sit against the wall or a door with your lower back pressed flat. There shouldn't be any space between your lower back and the wall. Slide down the wall until your knees are not quite at ninety degrees. If you feel pain in your knees, slide up a little higher on the wall. Your knees and feet should point straight ahead with your feet about two fist-widths apart. Make sure you walk your feet away from the wall far enough that your ankle bones are under or slightly in front of your knee joint. This exercise restores balance between the muscles of the legs, hips, and lumbar spine.

After this sequence, you should feel taller, lighter, and more balanced and experience a significant decrease in your stress levels—both postural and emotional.

# #3: SCAPULAR (SHOULDER BLADE) AND PELVIC DISPARITY

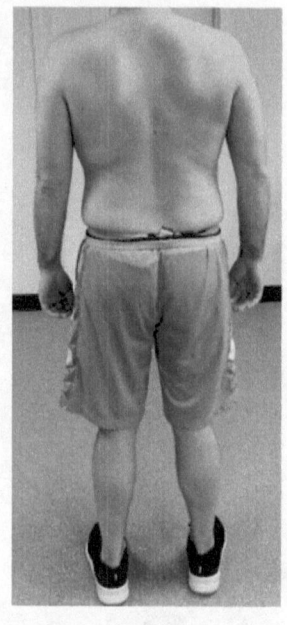
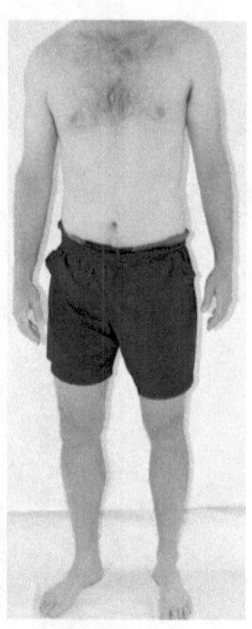

Fig. 1	Fig. 2	Fig. 3

*Fig. 1: The left hip from the back view is higher than the right, showing a hip disparity.*

*Fig. 2: The back view shows the right shoulder blade in a different position than the left and the right hip rotated forward. Notice the right foot in front of the left.*

*Fig. 3: The front view shows the right shoulder dropped, right hip elevated, and right foot turned out—all classic signs of hip and shoulder imbalance and disparity.*

Almost everyone has a positional or functional disparity (or both) in their shoulder blades and hips. In layman's terms, that means one shoulder and one hip are functioning differently or are positioned differently than the other, and it's creating a major muscle tension disparity from head to toe. How do you know this is you?

The first indication is if you have pain on one side of your body—one shoulder, hip, knee, one-sided back or neck pain, etc. Visually, when you're looking at yourself in the mirror, if you see one hand in front of your body more than the other, notice one shoulder is dropped lower, one side of your pelvis looks higher or closer to the mirror, one foot turns out or sits in front of the other, or any other difference between the right and left sides of your body, then this sequence is a great place to start.

It's important to understand that if one shoulder is in a different position or functioning differently from the other, then so is one hip. Shoulder imbalance *always* corresponds to an imbalance between hips without exception. Why? Because as soon as you change the position of one, you change the tension in the muscles of the spine, which connects the hip bone to the shoulder bones. Consequently, restoring one joint back to neutral alignment and function also often restores the other or, at the very least, improves it greatly. Keep in mind that your postural imbalances and your emotional stress don't usually have to shift much for the pain to improve a lot. In most cases, it just takes a very small shift to go a long way in terms of pain relief. In other words, you're not striving for perfection, because it isn't required. You're simply striving for better than it is now.

**Symptoms:** One-sided pain anywhere in your body, including pain on one side of the neck, back, shoulder, hip, knee, foot, and ankle. Meniscus tears, medial or lateral knee pain, disc bulges and herniations, sprained ankles, nerve pain, plantar fasciitis.

**Contraindications**: Skip any exercise that increases pain. Skip the assisted hip stretch if you have degenerative changes in your hip joint. This is a demanding sequence on the shoulder joint, so avoid pushing any exercise to the point of pain.

**Sequence:** Do the exercises in the order listed and pay close attention to your form.

## SITTING TRICEP STRETCH: 1 MINUTE EACH SIDE

Sit in a chair with your hips in the middle of the chair (not up against the backrest). Place a yoga block or a pillow from your couch between your knees and squeeze with moderate pressure. Roll the front of your hip bones forward to create an arch in your lower back. Keep your upper body upright—no leaning forward. Bend your right elbow, and place your right hand on your right shoulder. Place your left hand under your right elbow, and pull both elbows up overhead. You may feel a stretch in the back of your right arm or tricep muscle. After 1 minute, repeat the exercise with the opposite arm. This exercise is repositioning the upper back, restoring function to the shoulder joint and addressing the position of the shoulder blade.

## SINGLE ARM GLIDES:
## 2 SETS OF 10 REPS ON EACH ARM

Lie on your back with both legs up on a chair or couch, with your knees and hips as close to ninety degrees as possible. With both arms in the goalpost position, slide one hand straight up overhead while keeping your elbow and the back of your hand on the ground. Hold for 3 seconds, then bring the arm back to the starting position and repeat with the other arm. Alternate arms after each repetition. The key is to do your best to keep your elbows and the back of your hands on the ground. If you can't touch the ground with the back of your hand, just do the best you can without straining your shoulder. This exercise restores proper glide to the shoulder blade and helps to balance out the muscles of the spine.

## Assisted Hip Stretch: 1 Minute Each Side

Lie on your back and place both feet on a wall or a door, keeping your hips and knees bent at ninety degrees. Place one ankle across the opposite knee. Your tailbone should remain on the ground during the entire exercise. With your leg muscles (not your hand), push your knee toward the wall. You should feel a stretch in the back of your leg or hip. Hold for 1 minute, then switch legs. This exercise rebalances the hip muscles and realigns the pelvis.

## Supine Pillow Squeezes: 60 Repetitions

Lie on your back with your knees bent and feet flat on the ground. Your feet should be pointing straight ahead. Place a pillow between your knees and squeeze and release it at a medium pace and around 70 percent strength. You should squeeze the pillow with a rhythmic, pulsing motion. Place your arms out to your sides slightly below your shoulders with your palms up and relax your upper body. This exercise balances out the hip muscles and activates the muscles that stabilize the pelvis, hip, and knee.

## Downward Dog on Elbows and Knees: 1 Minute

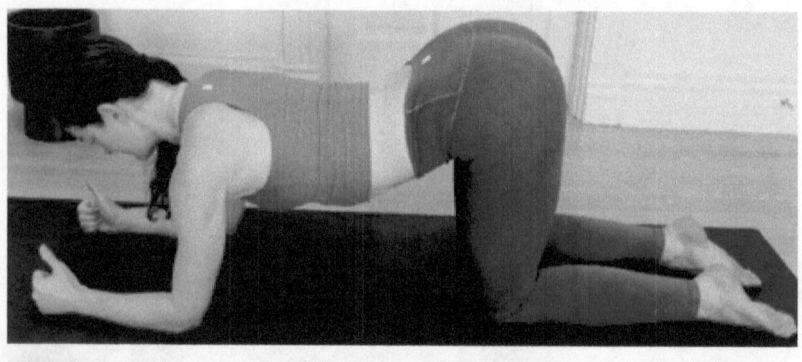

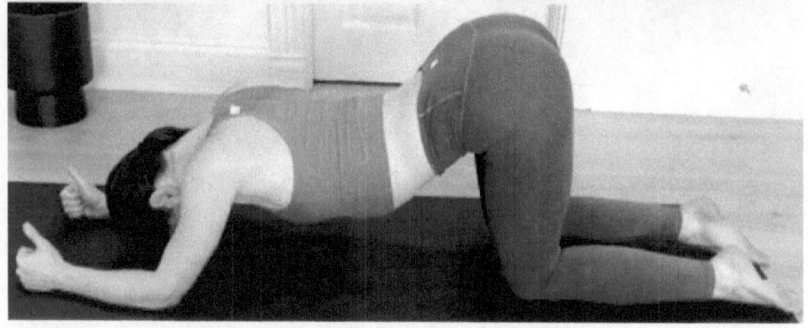

Begin with your elbows directly under your shoulders and your hips directly over your knees. Make a fist with your hands, thumbs up, and hands shoulder-width apart. Walk your elbows forward four to six inches. Drop your head, allow your shoulder blades to drop together, and pull your hips up and back toward your heels like you would in a regular downward dog. Keep your knees on the ground. Let your stomach drop toward the ground and allow your back to sway. You should feel work in your shoulder blades and upper back and possibly a slight stretch in your shoulders. Make sure to relax your head and neck completely by tucking your chin down toward your chest. This exercise realigns the mid and upper spine and reconnects the shoulders to the hips.

This sequence will help you feel more balanced in your feet and hips, and you might feel much taller than when you started!

## #4: SWAYED-FORWARD HIPS

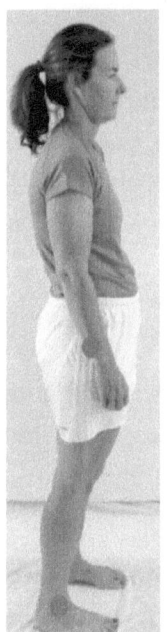
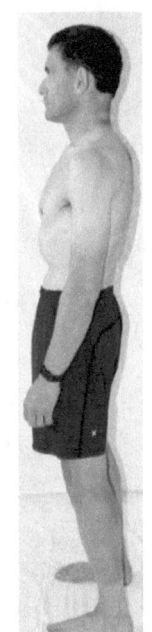

With swayed-forward hips, the hip joint lies in front of the ankle and the shoulder. The head almost always moves forward as the hips move forward, and the shoulders are usually rounded forward. The gravity line and dots help us see the relationship between the shoulders, hips, and ankles more easily.

If you found that your hips swayed forward of your shoulders while examining your posture from the side, then you probably need this sequence. The hip joint is designed to sit directly under the shoulder joint and above the knee joint. That way, as gravity travels through your body, it's distributed equally through the middle of each joint. When neutral alignment is present like this, the muscles on the front of the body are under equal tension with the muscles on the back side of the body. As soon as the hips sway forward, we can deduce several things:

1. The muscles that line the spine are out of balance with the abdominals.
2. The hip flexor muscles are out of balance with the hip extensors.
3. Gravity has been displaced behind the spine, creating an overload on the lower back and the base of the neck.
4. Diaphragmatic function is compromised.
5. Scapular (shoulder blade) function is likely compromised.

This posture often corresponds to a rounded upper back and forward shoulders. This is due to the fact that as the center of gravity (found above the hip joint) shifts forward, the spine counterbalances the weight distribution to maintain balance by shutting down the extensor muscles of the mid and upper back. The extensor muscles are the ones you use to pull your shoulders back. Strengthening them alone doesn't usually solve the pelvic muscle weakness that accompanies and usually causes the forward sway.

You'll notice the first postural condition we addressed was forward, rounded shoulders, but this particular condition deserves its own sequence because of the underlying hip and pelvic muscle imbalance.

**Symptoms:** Neck pain, jaw pain, headaches, migraines, TMJ, upper, mid, and lower back pain, anterior and posterior knee pain, patellar tendonitis, Achilles tendonitis, plantar fasciitis, back spasms.

**Contraindications:** Anything that instigates or increases pain.

**Sequence:** Do the exercises in the order listed and always try to follow the instructions on form.

## Downward Dog on Elbows and Knees: 1 Minute

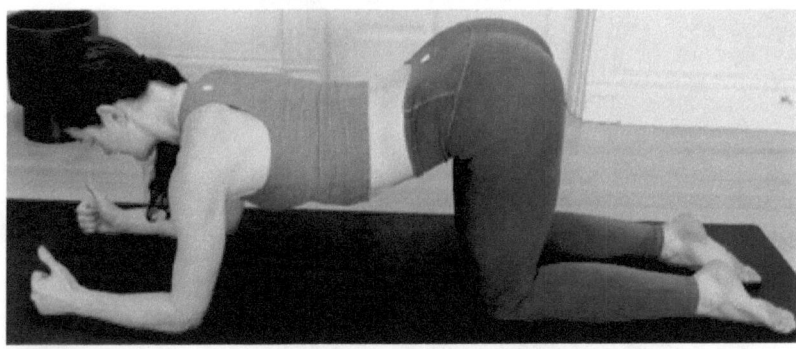

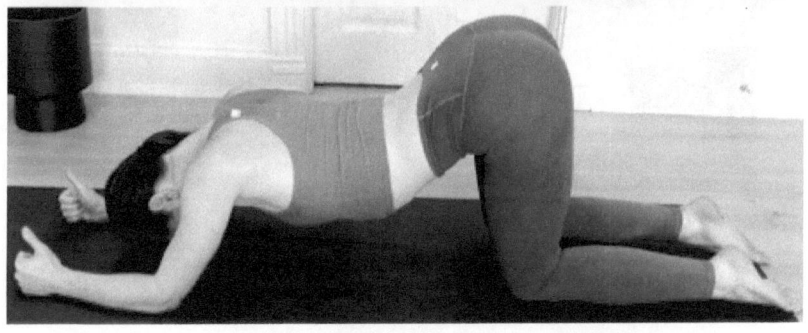

Begin with your elbows directly under your shoulders and your hips directly over your knees. Make a fist with your hands, thumbs up, and hands shoulder-width apart. Walk your elbows forward four to six inches. Drop your head, allow your shoulder blades to drop together, and pull your hips up and back toward your heels like you would in a regular downward dog. Keep your knees on the ground. Let your stomach drop toward the ground and allow your back to sway. You should feel work in your shoulder blades and upper back and possibly a slight stretch in your shoulders. Make sure to relax your head and neck completely by tucking your chin down toward your chest. This exercise realigns the mid and upper spine and reconnects the shoulders to the hips.

## Modified Low Back Stretch: 2 Minutes

Lie on your back with your feet on the wall and your ankles level with your knees. Your knees should be bent to around forty-five degrees (knees closer to your chest than ninety degrees). Squeeze your knees and your ankles together and hold for 2 minutes. Breathe deeply in and out through your nose. This exercise mildly stretches your lower back, activates the deep hip and spinal stabilizers, and realigns your upper back and shoulders.

## ACTIVE HIP STRETCH: 1 MINUTE

Lie on your back with your knees bent. Cross your right ankle over the opposite knee. Push your right knee away from you (with your leg muscles) while keeping your left knee and hip bent ninety degrees. Relax your arms out to your sides with your palms up. Relax your upper body completely. Do not hold your legs up with your arms. We want your hip and leg muscles to do all the work. Keep your lower back flat on the ground. This exercise stretches the deep muscles of the hips and activates the abdominals and spinal stabilizers.

## Chair Pose: 30 Seconds

Stand with your feet straight, about six inches apart. Bend your knees and lower your hips like you're sitting in a chair until you're in a squat position with your hips well above your knees. Spread your fingers out and raise your arms straight up overhead as high as you can comfortably raise them. Keep your palms facing each other. Lock out your elbows and point your thumbs back behind you. Look straight ahead and hold. This exercise helps to balance out the front and back sides of your body while activating all the important hip and scapular stabilizers.

## #5: DYSFUNCTIONAL HIP AND SPINAL MECHANICS

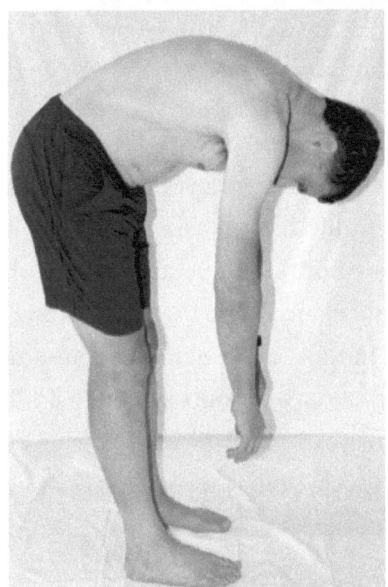

*Both these pictures depict the lack of lower back and hip joint function, not hamstring tightness. Hamstring tightness is a symptom and is secondary to hip and spinal mechanics 90 percent of the time.*

*Man squatting down showing functional hip, low back, knee, and ankle mechanics.*

I can say with confidence and years of experience to back me up that if you have chronic hip or back pain, you have a mechanical imbalance in one or both of these areas. The other sequences will also address these imbalances, but I wanted to provide a very specific sequence to restore motion and function, because you need as close to full function as possible to free yourself from pain. How do you know if this sequence is for you?

- You can't touch your toes or can't touch without bending your knees.
- You can't squat down to your heels.
- You've had a past ankle, knee, back, or hip injury.
- You have hip pain or back pain.

The hip joint might be the single most important joint in the body for you to ensure it has its full range of motion. The shoulder and the knee would be close seconds. Of course, the knee bone is the hip bone (the femur), so if the knee doesn't go to full extension—if it isn't able to be completely straight through the end phases of walking—then the hip won't reach it either.

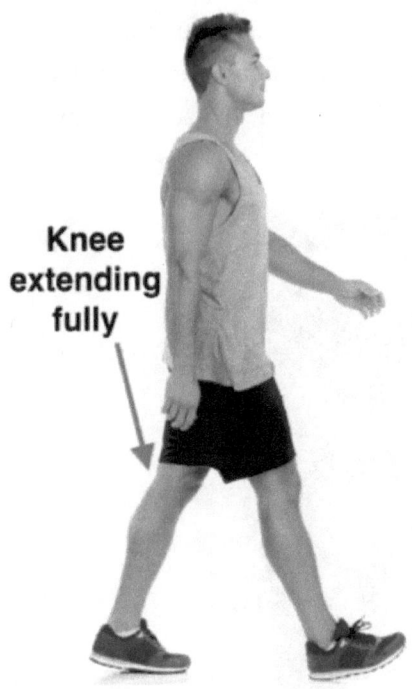

*Example of proper hip and knee mechanics when walking*

Proper functional mechanics of the knee, hip, and spine are very specific. When the ankle and knee bear the full weight of the body during walking, the knee should be moving toward, and eventually reach, as close to a "locked out" position (full extension) as possible. The femur should then be able to move independently within the hip joint to reach its end-range motion. All this time, the spine should remain still and stable.

If the knee doesn't straighten or the hip joint can't move unimpeded through its full range of motion, then the pelvis and spine have to compensate. They compensate by twisting or laterally shifting, which results in shear force on the spine and tightness in the hip muscles. Disc herniations, hip and spinal-joint tightness, degeneration, and arthritis are often the results.

On the other hand, if the hip and knee joints are functioning perfectly, but the lower back can't round forward all the way (flexion) or bend backward to its end-motion (extension), then the back muscles and spine will be compromised, and at risk of injury and deterioration.

*A woman bending with perfect spinal rounding (flexion), and a golfer with perfect back bend (extension) at the end of his drive. Also, notice the perfect right knee and hip extension on the golfer during his follow-through.*

No one that I know of in the traditional medical world will address your back pain or hip pain by helping you restore full knee extension. Nor will they usually focus on restoring full flexion and extension to your spine. Instead, they usually tell you to stretch and strengthen, neither of which is specific enough to pinpoint the actual problem. For instance, strengthening the spine when you can't bend over to touch your toes usually only makes it tighter. Stretching or strengthening your hips when they're tight doesn't address the underlying lack of knee function, and strengthening your core doesn't do anything except give you a nice workout.

By the end of this sequence, you should feel like you're closer to touching your toes, and your hips should move more freely.

**Symptoms:** Hip pain, degenerative hip joint, degenerative disc disease, stenosis, arthritis in the knee, spine, or hip, back spasms, back and hip muscle tightness, knee pain, and stiffness.

**Contraindications:** Skip any exercise that increases pain. Also, avoid the Wall Shoulder and Hamstring Stretch if you have a lower back disc herniation, shoulder pain, or sciatic nerve pain.

**Sequence:** Do the exercises in the order listed and pay close attention to form.

## Overhead Extension: 1 Minute

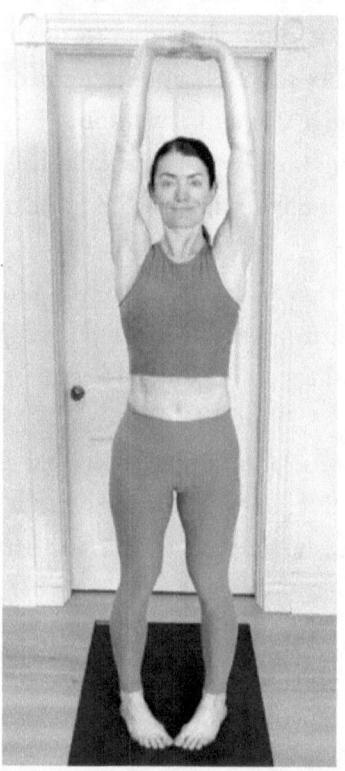

Stand with your big toes touching and your heels out (pigeon-toed). Keep the weight on the insides of your feet, lock out your knees, and contract your thigh muscles. Interlace your hands together and bring your arms straight up overhead while locking out your elbows. Push your palms toward the ceiling. Look straight ahead, drop your shoulders away from your ears, and relax your neck. Keep your hips over your ankles (don't let your hips sway forward). This exercise repositions the pelvis and the hip joint and aligns the major load-bearing joints.

## WALL SHOULDER AND HAMSTRING STRETCH: 1 MINUTE

Place your palms on the wall around chest-height. Walk your feet back and bend at the waist, keeping your hands in place. Relax your stomach and chest toward the floor and try to induce an arch in your lower back by rolling the front of your hip bones forward toward the ground. Your ankles should be directly under your hips, and your elbows should be locked out. Keep most of the weight in your legs. This exercise engages the entire back side of the body and restores the alignment between shoulders and hips.

## Standing Quadricep Stretch: 1 Minute

Stand with your foot behind you on a chair, table, or couch, or grab your foot behind you with your hand if you can. Keep your knees level and tuck your hips gently under to increase the stretch on the front of your thigh. Keep your knee straight on the down leg (don't let it bend) and keep your upper body straight up. This exercise restores function to the hip joint and reminds the hips of their role in bearing equal weight.

## Kneeling Hip Flexor Stretch: 1 Minute

Kneel on one knee and step forward into a lunge position with the opposite leg. Keep your upper body straight and sink your hips forward until you feel a stretch on the front of the trailing leg. Relax your shoulders. This exercise lengthens the muscles on the front of the hip and restores end-range motion to both hip joints.

## SPIDER LUNGE: 1 MINUTE

From a lunge position on one knee (see above exercise), place your hands on the inside of your foot and let your upper body relax toward the floor. Sink your hips down toward the ground and hold the position. Drop your chest toward the ground as much as comfortable. You might feel a stretch in both hips, inner thighs, or lower back. This exercise reminds the lower spine of its ability to flex while both hips move independently through flexion and extension.

## Downward Dog with Knees Bent: 1 Minute

Begin on your hands and knees with hands under your shoulders and knees under your hips. Bring your knees and hips up in the air as high as possible. Keep your knees slightly bent and pull your hips up and back toward your heels as you pull your chest toward your knees. Raise your heels slightly up off the floor and lock out your elbows. You want your spine to be aligned with your hands and shoulders (see previous image). This exercise restores functional mechanics to the hips and spine.

## Wall Sit: 1 Minute

Sit against the wall or a door and slide your hips down until your knees are not quite at ninety degrees. Press your lower back flat. There shouldn't be any space between your lower back and the wall. If you feel discomfort in your knees, slide up a little higher on the wall. Your knees and feet should point straight ahead with your feet about two fist-widths apart. Make sure you walk your feet away from the wall far enough that your ankle bones are under or are slightly in front of your knee joint. This exercise restores balance between the muscles of the hips and lumbar spine.

This sequence will help you bend lower as you touch your toes and will help you restore function to your hips and spine. You might also feel more balanced and taller after.

No matter which sequence you do, I have one word of caution: Pay attention. Connect to your body and stay tuned in to how it responds. If you're not paying attention to how each exercise affects you, you risk overdoing it or not finding relief.

Otherwise, have fun, and reap the benefits of being more aligned, balanced, connected, and, hopefully soon, free of pain.

Important reminders:

- Do the exercises in the order they appear.
- Follow the form closely.
- If you can only do the exercise for half the recommended duration or less, gradually increase it until you reach the full duration.
- If any sequence or exercise incites or increases pain, skip it and go to the next one.
- To start, do them daily. Once you're out of pain, you can continue to do them daily or several times a week.
- You can do any sequence once or twice a day as long as you pay attention to your body and don't overdo it.
- Do them anytime that works for you, whether in the morning, afternoon, or evening.
- Revisit any or all the routines throughout your life.
- If the pain doesn't abate, don't worry; it might be very emotionally rooted, or it might just take more time, in which case, there is still lots and lots of hope!

## Chapter 25

## 20,000 BREATHS OF LIFE

Now that you're on your way to more balance in body and mind, it's crucial to learn how to use the power of breath to enhance and support your health. The way we breathe is intimately tied to the quality of our health and to the experience of pain, but few people know exactly what proper breathing is. Most people have been told that by taking a few deep breaths a day, even several times a day, they're providing sufficient oxygen to the body and relieving stress, which is true for a limited time.

While deep breathing is certainly helpful, ten good breaths sometimes aren't enough to counteract the constant stream of stress and worry, and the other roughly 20,000 dysfunctional (and unconscious) breaths most of us take during a normal day.

After all, breathing is an autonomic process, which means our body regulates it for us. Once you're finished breathing your ten to twenty purposeful, conscious breaths (if that's even something you practice), you go about your day and return to breathing as you always have, which means most people return to their shallow, limited breathing patterns that starve the brain and body of the plentiful and necessary oxygen they need to thrive.

Therefore, to maximize the other thousands of breaths, three things need to change:

1. Your posture
2. Your stress levels
3. The way you breathe

Posture is intimately tied to your ability to breathe optimally. When we inhale, our rib cage expands as each of the twelve ribs rotate upward and out. This expansion is possible due to the connection of the ribs on the spine.

Two conditions are required for the rib cage to expand completely in order to fully oxygenate the blood:

1. A flexible, functional spine
2. Pliable, balanced muscles and fascia surrounding the rib cage

In perfect, optimal inhalation, the internal and external intercostal muscles that surround and attach to the rib cage contract, drawing the rib cage up and expanding the thoracic cavity as the diaphragm descends. This expansion creates a pressure differential between the inside air and the outside air, causing the outside air to rush into the lungs, where oxygen is absorbed into the bloodstream and carried to every cell in the body.

As the cells take in oxygen, they unload waste products back into the blood. When we exhale, the rib cage lowers, the diaphragm expands, and some of these waste products, like carbon dioxide, are expelled. When we're breathing optimally, we are under the control of our parasympathetic nervous systems (rest-and-relax mode), which is our natural state of balance and harmony.

Then, there's a state of disharmony. The two most important structures while breathing are the rib cage and the diaphragm, both of which can be severely impeded when the muscles that attach to the pelvis and the spine are too tight, too weak, or too imbalanced. Under those conditions, the pelvis, the spine, and the shoulders lose their ability to move freely. As a result, they can inhibit the ability of the rib cage and diaphragm to expand and descend completely. That leads to a partial breath rather than a full breath, which is how most adults breathe.

Without a full inhalation, less oxygen is absorbed into the blood, all the cells of the body produce less energy, our metabolic rate changes, and we become tired or lethargic. When there's limited inhalation, there's also limited exhalation to the point that all the carbon dioxide waste may not be completely expelled.

Carbon dioxide is slightly acidic, so to maintain a balanced pH in the blood, the brain increases our rate of respiration to increase oxygen levels and decrease carbon dioxide. Heart rate increases as breath rate increases, kicking in our sympathetic nervous system (fight-or-flight), thereby mimicking the very conditions our bodies experience when we're under stress.

Essentially, our bodies and brains become stuck in survival mode, and true relaxation isn't possible until we sit upright and consciously take deep, fulfilling breaths. At that point, our shoulders can relax, our stress levels decrease, and our bodies come back into balance. Then, we unconsciously go about the rest of our day doing the same things that created all this disharmony in the first place.

So, if posture is the key to optimal breathing, and breathing is the key to providing energy to our bodies and cells and to decreasing stress, then restoring ideal posture is paramount to managing stress levels and restoring optimal health.

In my many years as a postural therapist, I noticed a great number of people who have rounded, forward shoulders and immobile, thoracic spines. They also have misaligned necks, which can tighten the muscles on the front of the neck and obstruct the airway to varying degrees.

Try this experiment: Purposely round your shoulders and upper back forward and take a deep breath. You'll notice immediately how difficult it is to take in a full, complete breath. Then, sit or stand upright, pull your shoulders back a bit, and take a deep breath. It's a completely different experience. You can actually breathe.

Short, limited, and rapid breathing, similar to what you just experienced with your shoulders hunched, is the body's fear mode. Many people with this posture are stuck in fear, worry, and anxiety, for which their posture is at least partially responsible.

Before we restore proper breathing posture, we also need to

understand *how* to breathe, which brings up the question of whether we should breathe through our nostrils or more through our mouths.

In James Nestor's book *Breath: The New Science of a Lost Art*, he writes, ". . . Scientists discovered that 90 percent of us—very likely me, you, and almost everyone you know—is breathing incorrectly and that this failure is either causing or aggravating a laundry list of chronic diseases."

Take a deep breath in and out through your mouth and notice the duration of your inhalation and exhalation. Then, take a deep breath in and out through your nose and notice the duration of your breath cycle.

You should have discovered that breathing through your mouth was very shallow, and the duration of the whole cycle was much faster than breathing through your nose. That makes sense, considering our nasal passages are specifically dedicated to breathing, while our mouths are more suited for eating and talking.

As we inhale through the nose, our nasal passages help filter out foreign particles and moisten the air, making the air more readily usable to our lungs. Nasal breathing also slows down the flow of air into the lungs, enhancing the oxygenation of the blood, allowing our lungs time to expand fully and the diaphragm time to descend fully. As we nose-breathe, nitric oxide molecules are also released into the lungs, which act as messengers to widen blood vessels, decrease blood pressure, increase oxygen uptake, and boost immune function, among other things.

Those are only the benefits of prolonged inhalation through the nose. There are also multiple benefits to breathing out through the nose. One of those benefits is prolonged exhalation, which further calms the nervous system, expels waste products more completely, and helps us exit the near-constant fight-or-flight mode so we can shift back into the rest-and-relax mode.

Unfortunately, most people mouth-breathe throughout their day, which Nestor and other breathing scientists have shown leads to an increase in blood pressure, respiratory infections, and fatigue while decreasing endurance, mental clarity, and overall energy.

The benefits of nose-breathing and the detriments of mouth-breathing have been touted for millennia from ancient texts to Tibetan monks, Native Americans, and modern yogis. It seems the common theme from all of them, learned and passed down over centuries, is that a habit of breathing from your mouth is very bad for your health.

Deep breathing, in general, has been shown to have several beneficial effects, including:

- Decreased stress
- Improved cognitive function
- Improved lung health
- Decreased blood pressure
- The release of endorphins
- Stimulation of the immune system
- Regulation of blood PH
- Promotion of calm, clarity, and self-connection
- Increased uptake of oxygen to the muscles, brain, and organs
- Pain relief
- Improved digestion

This is just a small sample of the benefits of taking the time to breathe deeply on a daily basis.

So, in order to breathe properly, reap some (or all) of these benefits, and begin to address the inner and outer conditions that might be keeping you in pain, let's do some posture and breathing exercises.

## Exercise and Breathing Sequence

This movement and breathing sequence will open up your upper back and chest while freeing up your rib cage and your diaphragm. You can do it once a day for a while or several times a day. Whether you believe you breathe perfectly already or not, freeing up your body and improving your posture can only help.

## Kneeling Shoulder and Chest Stretch: 1 Minute

While on your knees, place your elbows on the seat of a chair or couch with your elbows bent ninety degrees and hands resting on your forearms. Rest your forehead on the chair and walk your knees back until they're directly underneath your hips. Let your chest and stomach relax and drop toward the ground. You might feel a stretch in your chest, your shoulders, or both. Relax your spine and let your lower back form an arch. This exercise repositions the mid and upper back, releases the tight muscles in your chest, stomach, and underarms, and reconnects the spinal muscles from top to bottom.

## SUPINE UPPER SPINAL TWIST: 1 MINUTE, EACH SIDE

Lie on one side with your knees and hips at ninety degrees. Your knees and ankles should be stacked on top of each other. Without letting your knees come apart or the top knee slide off the bottom knee, open your top arm up and over toward the opposite side with your palm facing up toward the ceiling. Let your head relax on the ground. If needed, you can place a pillow under your head to keep your neck comfortable. Breathe deeply in and out through your nose and allow your mid and upper back to relax. You might feel a stretch across your chest, on your sides, or in your back. This exercise restores motion and function to the spine while opening up the chest and realigning your upper back.

## CATS AND DOGS: 10 TIMES IN EACH DIRECTION

With your hands under your shoulders and knees under your hips, round your spine up toward the ceiling as far as possible with your head down, then roll your spine the opposite way. As your back arches (picture on the right), allow your shoulder blades to drop together and look up toward the ceiling.

## STATIC RESTING POSITION: 5 MINUTES

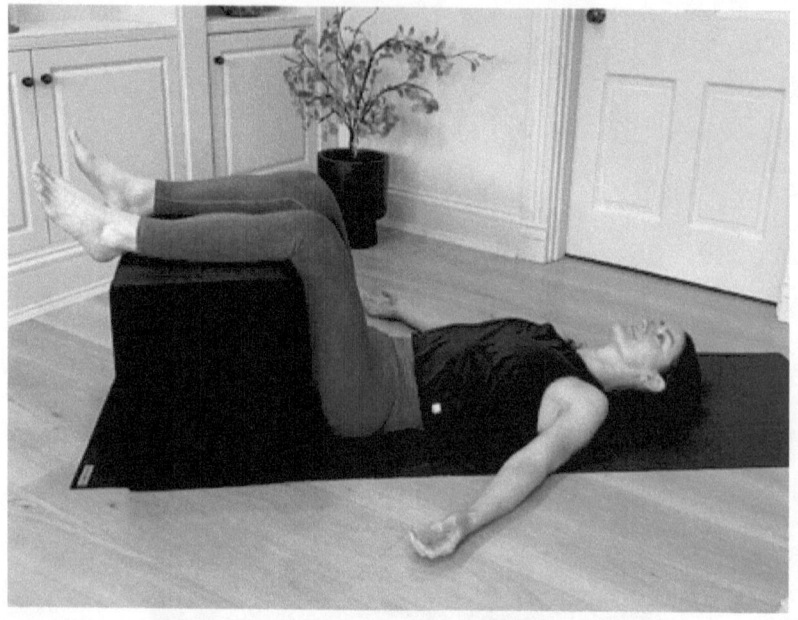

Lying on your back with your knees and hips at ninety degrees and knees resting on a chair or couch. Your palms should be up and your arms out to your sides below your shoulders. Relax your neck, lower back, and your hips. There should be no muscle tension in your body here. Breathe deeply in and out through your nose. This exercise realigns the entire spine, balances out the muscles that surround the spine, and enables the back muscles to relax.

In all four of these exercises, breathe deeply in through your nose, hold for two seconds, then breathe out slowly and completely through your nose until you've expelled all the air in your lungs and your stomach. Breathe slowly and methodically. Take five to ten breaths in each position. As you breathe, consciously release and relax your shoulders, neck, hips, and knees.

Make sure you focus on the exhale as much as or more than the inhale. The more air you push out of your lungs, the more you force the diaphragm to expand, enabling a stronger inhale on the rebound.

You'll notice that just one session of this movement and breathing sequence will dramatically change your body and your stress levels. As you repeat the sequence daily, and as your shoulders and upper back free up, you'll begin to breathe easier throughout the day while also standing more upright. You'll also decrease the amount of stress on your body and free up energy for your other organs, muscles, and immune system so they can function more effectively and efficiently.

## Shut up and Walk

One of the best ways to improve your lung capacity and your cardiovascular conditioning is to walk, hike, or even jog with your mouth purposely closed. This isn't exactly social hour, but keeping your mouth shut will force you to breathe through your nose and will activate your diaphragm immediately. As you breathe that way for longer periods, climb hills, or jog slowly, your body will begin to feel starved for oxygen. This will cause your brain to think it needs to be more efficient with the body's oxygen uptake and can lead to a boost in red blood cells and hemoglobin. It's similar to how the body responds at high altitudes.

Make sure you can still breathe, though, and bring some tissue or a hanky in case you need to clear your nostrils. Do this a few times a week for ten to fifteen minutes during a hike or a very slow jog. Like anything, the more you practice, the easier it will become, so don't be discouraged if you can only do a few minutes at a time to start.

## Chapter 26

# VISUALIZING THE GOLD

If you've ever watched the Olympics, then you've seen snowboarders, ski jumpers, sprinters, long jumpers, and other athletes rehearse their performance in their heads ahead of time. They visualize the gold medal routine right before the event in order to pre-condition their brains to perform exactly the right movements. This has been a tried, tested, and proven technique to improve athletic performance for decades.

Lindsay Vonn, one of the greatest downhill skiers of all time, believed visualization gave her a leg up on the competition. She would physically create her performance ahead of time by shifting her body from right to left and front to back as she visualized passing each gate.

But athletes and Olympians aren't the only ones who use it. Actors Jim Carrey and Will Smith both imagined themselves as massive stars ahead of time. Carrey even wrote himself a ten-million-dollar check dated several years in the future before he had a dime to his name and carried it in his wallet for years until he was paid exactly ten million for his role in *Dumb and Dumber*.

Oprah Winfrey is famous for using visualization boards to lay out her ideal life ahead of time. Her advice to others was to "Create the highest, grandest vision possible for your life because you become what you believe."

However, visualization goes beyond just goal-setting. When you visualize the outcome ahead of time and make it real by bringing in all your senses, feeling the emotions, feeling your muscles contracting and reacting, and imagining the people you're with and the place you're in, you're programming your brain to make those things a reality. In fact, you're living it in your head as if it already was real.

It works because your brain doesn't distinguish between what's real on the outside versus what's imagined on the inside. Take dreams, for example. They seem completely real when you're in them. You actually believe you're riding a red Tyrannosaurus rex through the streets of San Francisco, as I dreamed one time, or soaring through the air like an eagle looking down at the clouds underneath you.

I was once on a plane dreaming that I was playing tennis. As I hit a winning backhand, my arm flew in the air and whacked the guy sitting next to me in the chest. It woke me up immediately. Obviously, my body didn't know the difference between hitting a backhand in my mind compared to doing it on a real tennis court. The guy next to me did, though. When I looked over at him to apologize, it was clear he was dreaming of throwing me off the plane.

Clearly, visualizing has value in athletics and life, but how does all that relate to health?

Several years ago, I got off a ski lift and bent over to buckle my boots before going down the slope. My sister didn't see my ski and accidentally skied over my right ski, which caught on hers and pulled my legs out like I was going into the splits. To avoid tearing my groin muscles, I fell on my side, but because my boot was locked into my ski, I ended up tearing one of the ligaments in my knee and taking out a small chunk of cartilage off the bone.

I didn't need surgery for the ligament, but the doctors wanted to do a complicated and lengthy surgery to repair the cartilage in my knee, which would have kept me off that leg for months, followed by a lengthy recovery that would have lasted up to a year. Even then, the chances of success were not guaranteed. Needless to say, I elected not to do the surgery, believing there had to be another way and trusting that I would find one. Three months later, I was walking and playing tennis normally again, but if I played or ran too much, my knee would complain.

Frustrated that I hadn't fully healed, I decided I needed to change things up, so I did two things: First, I decided to completely rest it for three weeks, where all I did was walk. I didn't do any running, tennis, or strength training. Next, I began to visualize myself running and playing tennis with no pain. I would go on a run in my mind and feel my muscles contracting as my feet hit the ground. I imagined running without pain or limitation.

After my run, which lasted just a few minutes, I imagined playing tennis where I was running and cutting and changing directions and going all out at 100 percent, all the while feeling my muscles contract, the court underneath my feet, and my knee free of pain. I did this every day for about five minutes a day.

When I returned to activity three weeks later, I was a completely new man. I had turned the corner to the point that I suddenly was able to play multiple days in a row, strength train without pain, and run long distances without my knee complaining.

There are mounds of scientific evidence backing up the power of visualization and its effect on the body, but let me highlight a few of them to prove the point.

In one particular study, the goal was to measure improvements in bicep strength (the muscle on the front of the arm that bends the elbow), so they had one group do nothing, another group visualize strengthening their bicep muscles only, a third group strength train only, and a fourth group both visualize and strength train.

It turned out that the group that only visualized their arms getting stronger made significant strength gains far exceeding the control group that did nothing. The group that both visualized and strength-trained increased their bicep strength the most by far compared to all the other groups, including the group that strength-trained only.

Another study published in the *Journal of Neuroscience* measured neural activity in the brain using an MRI while people were doing finger exercises. They found that whether people actually performed the exercises or just imagined doing them, the brain's motor cortex was activated equally.

These are two of many examples of how our bodies follow and respond to our imaginations and desires.

Visualization works because picturing what you want before you have it makes your brain come up with answers on how to get it and preconditions your nervous system as if it's already happened. Essentially, you make pain a vestige of the past while constructing a present, pain-free reality in your mind.

Also, if you remember what you learned about the biological relationship between the mind and body, then you know that your thoughts and feelings trigger a release of chemical compounds that circulate through every single cell. That means you actually have the power to influence your capacity to heal in accordance with your imagination and your will.

Hopefully, this fact empowers you to begin consciously and purposely envisioning the health and life you desire.

Take the time and do it now. Close your eyes, and whatever challenging pain or health condition you're experiencing, visualize yourself doing the things you want to do and living the life you want to live without pain or limitation.

Imagine yourself feeling better than 100 percent and thriving. While you do it, feel your body moving, smell the air, put yourself completely in the moment, and make it as real as you possibly can, as if you were actually there. Science shows that the more real you make it, the more your brain responds to make it a reality.

Do this every day for five or ten minutes and reap the benefits of calming your mind while downloading new software that reprograms your brain and your body to follow a new pattern of health.

Next, in addition to visualizing optimal health, it's time you started feeling like you had it, too.

## Chapter 27

## CONSCIOUSLY CREATING OPTIMAL HEALTH

You now have multiple tools at your disposal to create the space for your body to heal, including exercises to balance your body, enhance your breathing, and improve energy levels, as well as meditations and techniques to address present and past emotional stress.

The last piece of the puzzle is to begin to consciously create higher emotional states like love and gratitude, which, according to science, have the potential to quantifiably shift your body toward better health. They can also transform your life.

You know how impactful your emotions are on your body. They can help you create either a positive biochemical environment that enriches your cells, upregulates your immune system, and promotes healing, or they can create a constricting environment where aches, pains, and illnesses can thrive. Therefore, rather than letting years of past conditioning, habits, and minor or major emotional trauma dictate your physical and emotional health, you can purposely and consciously create an inner environment that's much more conducive to the life and health you desire.

You can begin with gratitude. The word gratitude comes from the Latin word *gratia*, which means grace, gratefulness, and graciousness. It's often confused with being thankful. Gratitude is more than that, though. Its essence embodies a mix of emotions, including love, appreciation, vulnerability, thankfulness, surrender, and connection. It also has the power to change us in a multitude of meaningful ways.

There is an abundance of scientific research on gratitude that paints a picture of just how impactful it can be. Here are some relevant highlights:

- People who regularly experience gratitude feel healthier, have better psychological health, experience less stress, anxiety, and depression, and are generally happier than those who don't.
- Gratitude can improve empathy, self-esteem, and relationships and help people overcome trauma.
- Gratitude enhanced the feeling of emotional and mental strength while improving a sense of resilience in the wake of the 9/11 attacks.
- Subjects who kept a daily journal for just ten weeks listing things they were grateful for actually exercised more, were more optimistic, and felt better about their lives than the control subjects.
- That same group also had fewer visits to physicians than the subjects who focused on sources of aggravation rather than gratitude.
- Subjects who wrote letters of gratitude to someone in their lives who had never before been properly acknowledged and thanked for their kindness immediately exhibited a huge increase in happiness scores, and that happiness lasted for at least a month.
- Gratitude lights up the brain's reward pathways, can boost serotonin, and activates the brain stem to release dopamine (the neurotransmitter responsible for feeling pleasure).
- A study on couples found that taking the time to express gratitude for a partner enhanced their feelings of positivity toward them while also improving their ability to express their concerns about the relationship.

- Managers who expressed gratitude for their employees' work found that their employees worked harder and were up to 50 percent more productive.
- Gratitude helps people feel more positive emotions, relish good experiences, improve their health, deal with adversity, and build strong relationships.

To sum up, your health, well-being, resilience, relationships, self-esteem, emotional and mental strength, and happiness will all improve by regularly focusing on more gratitude in your life. Given the evidence, I think you'd agree that taking five or ten minutes out of your day to immerse yourself in something that can radically improve your life is worth it.

## Self-Love

Next on the list of emotions you want to cultivate for better health is self-love. Loving in general will do the trick as well, but similar to gratitude, science has proven that regularly letting in self-love will improve your body chemistry, raise your resonance and energy, and even shift your brain waves like you're in a state of meditation, which is where the real healing begins. Some of the other evidence-based health benefits of loving yourself include:

- Improved mental health
- Higher self-esteem and self-acceptance
- Better sleep
- Less worry and anxiety
- Increased motivation
- Higher self-awareness
- Better immunity
- More compassion for others
- More self-defined boundaries

These are just a few of the benefits, but there are many more. As emotional toxicity in the form of anger, fear, shock, and hurt is replaced by emotional luminosity in the form of love and gratitude, every cell that makes up our bodies can bathe in a new and infinitely more nourishing atmosphere. Finally, the more you love yourself, the closer you come to ending self-punishment in all forms, especially if it manifests as illness, injury, or pain. The best part about these emotions is they're easy to feel. You just have to practice.

Every morning, shortly after I wake up, I spend several minutes feeling gratitude for my wife, dog, house, health, parents, friends, family, and neighbors, my ability to help others create more fulfilling lives through better physical and emotional health, the people who helped me explore and develop that ability, and so much more.

Sometimes, I choose to focus on a few of those people and aspects of my life; other times, I spend time in gratitude toward all of them and extend that gratitude to the world around me, including the earth and the planet itself. It's a fantastic way to begin the day.

It isn't always easy, though. Sometimes, I wake up with a million things on my mind, including various worries, fears, doubts, irritations, and to-do's. Those are the days I first have to feel whatever comes up and allow those feelings to pass through me before reaching true gratitude.

I *always* reach it, though, because I consciously choose to. I know what my life feels like and looks like when I don't shift out of all the clutter, because I lived it most of my life. The clutter can be motivating in some ways, in that it can kick me out of bed and get me moving toward accomplishment, but it feels so much better to be motivated out of enthusiasm and excitement.

Now, it's your turn. I highly recommend doing this meditation every single day if you can. If that sounds too daunting, then aim to do it a few times a week to start. In whatever way you decide to practice gratitude or love, stay with the feeling for as long as you can. Five, ten, or twenty minutes isn't nearly too much, and no amount of time spent is too little unless you skip it altogether.

## The Light of Gratitude

Imagine a soft light glowing in the middle of your chest. This is the light of gratitude. See its radiance and feel its warmth inside you. Now, see and feel that light expanding throughout your chest and your abdomen, down into your hips, then your legs, then your feet. All the while, let the feeling of gratitude expand as the light grows. Let it extend up into your shoulders, your arms and hands, and up into your neck and head. Feel the love, the appreciation, the connection, and the energy of gratitude throughout your whole body.

Feel gratitude for your health, your life, and your opportunity to grow. Feel grateful for your beating heart that keeps you alive, for your lungs that bring your entire body oxygen, and for your brain that allows you to think and to be you.

Now let that light expand beyond your body and into the outside world. Let it connect to your significant other and to your close friends and feel your gratitude toward them. Then connect that light to siblings, parents, friends, coworkers, or whomever you wish to be grateful for and feel the gratitude as the light touches them. Expand into your neighborhood, then your city, then your state, and keep expanding it out into the world as far as you can imagine. Sit in gratitude for all people, all beings, and all things. Feel the connection, the appreciation, the thankfulness, and the love.

Spend as long as you can in the feeling of gratitude. Any amount of daily gratitude can shift your body chemistry and impact your life, but the more you let in, the bigger the shift. As you practice this feeling meditation every day, you'll continue to bring in more emotion, depth, love, and gratitude, and it can change you in ways you can't yet imagine.

It has transformed my life. I'm more connected to others

when I'm with them, less stressed throughout my day, and I no longer hold onto anger or blame. I also feel noticeably happier to be alive. Not that I wasn't happy about it before, but I have a different awareness and appreciation for everything and everyone in my life, and you can too.

## Loving Meditation

This meditation is similar to one for gratitude, only you're going to let the love in for yourself—especially your indomitable spirit, courage, compassion, intelligence, inner beauty, and talent. Remember to include love for your body, especially the areas that are hurting. They're not trying to betray you; they're simply speaking to you. Listen to what they have to say with unconditional love and let them be heard.

Close your eyes and focus on loving yourself for three minutes. Breathe deeply, and as you do, bring in as much love for yourself as you can muster. You can do it the same way you did for gratitude: Imagine a deep, powerful, glowing light in the middle of your chest that represents the feeling of pure, unconditional love. Let it expand to your entire body and sit with the feeling.

That's it. There's nothing complicated or elaborate about it. It doesn't need to be. You just need to feel. This is how you can meditate on gratitude, love, wonder, beauty, passion, intimacy, and every other emotion you wish to experience. Close your eyes, bring up the emotion, and stay with it for as long as you can.

## Loving Your Other Selves

I also highly recommend a similar meditation to love yourself as a child, adolescent, and young adult. Simply imagine you're in a safe space and bring in a younger version of yourself. Hold that child or teenager tight. Tell them how loveable they are, how you love them deeply and unconditionally, and that they'll never be alone. Feel their weight, the softness of their skin, their warm breath on your chest, and their loving embrace. Hold them as long as you'd like.

Your child and adolescent selves were never loved enough, no matter how loving your parents were. Now, they can be. You can be their source of unconditional love, and you can be your own, too.

All radical change and emotional healing come from aligning more fully with your true self, the part of you beyond the fear and pain, the part that knows you are absolutely, unconditionally loved.

## Epilogue

# A NEW PATH TO HEALING

CHANGE CAN BE challenging. Yet, most people don't change until the pain of staying the same becomes more than the pain of changing. I assume you've read this far because you may have reached that breaking point, and you're ready to make a shift in your body and your life. So, allow me to offer some suggestions on how you might incorporate some of what you've learned.

All of the tools you've acquired here have the potential to transform you and free you from chronic pain. If incorporating them all at once seems daunting, then start by choosing one or two that resonate with you the most. There isn't a right or wrong way to add them into your life, so I encourage you to adopt what you can in whatever way feels right.

No two people are the same, so it follows that no two daily routines are exactly the same. Some people I work with choose to meditate and breathe shortly after waking up. Some begin their day with coffee, drive the kids to school, and then take twenty or thirty minutes before work to visualize, breathe, and do their exercises. A few of my clients wake up and do their exercises, then meditate and breathe after work to destress from the day. One of my clients rarely does the exercises but began meditating and journaling a few days a week, and she says it's changed her life.

However you do it, it's crucial to remember that something has to shift in your thoughts and habits for your body to mirror that shift. Nothing will change without you changing first. You *can* change, though, if you incorporate these tools and hold the conviction that you will no longer tolerate anything less than optimal health.

In the meantime, I hope you've enjoyed the book and that:

You'll choose to abandon your old beliefs about aging, genetics, and health and adopt new, empowering ones that will serve you for years to come.

You'll commit to feeling your emotions purposely and deeply.

You'll consider alternative therapies when they make sense.

You recognize that your emotions dictate your life experience and that you can consciously create the very emotions you wish to feel in your body and in your life.

The next time you're sick or in pain, you'll consider looking inward to explore your why.

You'll decide to be the guardian of your thoughts, turn away from toxicity in more areas of your life, and choose to love yourself more and more every day.

You acknowledge that your mind and body aren't separate; they are the same, and they are you.

You remember that you can influence and even change your thoughts, feelings, habits, and emotions at any time. This means you can massively influence and improve your biochemistry consciously and purposely.

Finally, I want to leave you with a message of hope. As you align your body and free yourself from the constricting physical and emotional energies that have bound you for far too long, you create the space for your body to heal. After all, you are hardwired to heal at every level of your being, which means the cure is inside you, waiting for just the right nudge to come alive.

## A Moment of Gratitude

I WANT TO express my sincere gratitude for the sensational and selfless mentors and people in my life, without whom this book would not exist.

Chris Andersonn, your guidance, love, and insight can't be matched or repaid. Thank you for your friendship and unwavering support over the last thirty years and counting. I learn more about myself every day because of you.

Pete Egoscue, I owe you more than I can express for passing on not only your anatomical wisdom but also your deep compassion for those struggling with pain. You ignited a fire inside me and many others that burns brighter every day, which proves that your legacy is only just beginning.

Teresa, thank you for your nourishing love, tireless support, and enthusiastic encouragement. And thanks for being the perfect model. Every day, I learn something new from you about how to be more compassionate and aware. To that end, I promise not to wake you up every day at 4 a.m. with a new idea for a book.

John Freeman, editor extraordinaire, thank you once again for all your encouragement, advice, and expertise. Most of all, thank you for helping me continue to learn how to write. To quote my favorite *Enter the Dragon* line, "Your skill is extra-ordinary!"

Bill Stump, you are simply amazing. I am deeply grateful for your experience, editing, insight, knowledge, and support over the years for me, my career, and both books. Your suggestions made this book a thousand times better.

John Koehler, thank you for helping me bring both this book and *Ageless, Painless Tennis* into the world. I deeply appreciate your work and that of your talented team.

Kelly and Richard, you both have been tireless supporters, cheerleaders, models, travel and ski partners, Aperol spritz companions, and so much more. Thank you for your essential contributions to this book and the last.

To perhaps the most influential mentors throughout my life, my four parents—Bruce, Anndel, Margaret, and Keith—thank you for being incredible human beings, role models, friends, and my biggest supporters. I have no doubt you'll be the first to buy this book even after I've given you one. I love and appreciate you all more than you know.

Finally, to all my clients over the years, I owe you perhaps my deepest gratitude for teaching me way more than I taught you. Thank you for your trust, vulnerability, and willingness to let me be a part of your lives.

www.ingramcontent.com/pod-product-compliance
Lightning Source LLC
LaVergne TN
LVHW091541070526
838199LV00002B/160